STAIRSCAPING

STAIRSCAPING

A GUIDE TO BUYING, REMODELING, AND DECORATING INTERIOR AND EXTERIOR STAIRCASES

GLOUCESTER MASSACHUSETTS

QUARRY BOOKS

Andrew Karre

First published in the United States of America by:

Quarry Books, a member of
Quayside Publishing Group
33 Commercial Street
Gloucester, Massachusetts 01930-5089
Telephone: (978) 282-9590
Fax: (978) 283-2742
www.rockpub.com

Library of Congress Cataloging-in-Publication Data
Karre, Andrew.
    Stairscaping : a guide to buying, remodeling, and decorating interior and exterior staircases /Andrew Karre.
        p.   cm.
    ISBN 1-59253-204-7 (pbk.)
    1. Staircases. I. Title.
NA3060.K36 2005
721'.832—dc22   2005010367
                                                                    CIP

ISBN 1-59253-204-7

10 9 8 7 6 5 4 3 2 1

Design: Collaborated, Inc.
Cover Image: Brian Vanden Brink/Tony DiGregorio, Architect
Illustrations by Robert Leanna II

Printed in Singapore

This book is dedicated to all the people who worked so hard to put it together and to my wife, who always believed I could finish it.

–AK

CONTENTS

INTRODUCTION

If you've ever paused to admire a set of stairs or ever appreciated the feeling of a well-worn railing, then this is a book for you. If your own home has a staircase that doesn't seem to work as well as it should—or look as good as you would like—this is a book for you. A staircase can be a house's most distinctive and useful feature. In the pages that follow, you'll find example after example of this in some of the finest and most innovative staircases in houses of today and yesterday. As you find inspiration and ideas in the photographs, the text and illustrations will explain what works well about these magnificent stairs, giving you insight into how to build, revamp, or redecorate your own staircase.

It's a marvelous time for home design and construction. Many of the best construction methods and styles of the past are being reborn and reimagined by today's architects and builders. At the same time, the very latest in modern materials are making things possible in construction that were hardly imaginable only decades ago. In short, there's no excuse for a boring staircase.

PART I

Home Staircases

ONE

WHAT'S IN A STAIRCASE?

Stairs occupy a unique place in our homes. Functionally, they are little more than hallways between floors, a convenient way to get from point A to point B. Emotionally, however, a staircase can be vastly more than the sum of rise and run calculations, framing lumber, wallboard, and trim. Stairs serve a wide range of practical and emotional needs.

Means to an End

Of course, stairs do provide a way to get from one floor to the next without difficulty. Just try to imagine Scarlett O'Hara making a grand entrance by climbing down a ladder in *Gone with the Wind*. Stairs allow people to descend deliberately, gracefully, in easy defiance of gravity, as they look over everyone and everything else in the room. If it's hard to imagine Scarlett climbing down a ladder, it's equally hard to imagine her simply walking through a door. It just wouldn't do. There is no grander way to make an entrance—or an exit—than on a flight of stairs.

Stairs are fertile ground for the creative imagination. Aside from the countless architects and designers who have expressed themselves in staircases, artists in other media have often been enchanted by stairs. One need only look to the ever-shifting maze of stairs at Hogwarts School of Witchcraft and Wizardry in the Harry Potter books or to the mind-boggling endless stairs of artist M. C. Escher for evidence.

Stairs also serve humbler purposes. They're a place to plop down and think after a long day. They're the temporary home of the laundry basket bound for an upstairs bedroom. For kids, they're an impromptu jungle gym and, if lucky, an excellent vantage point from which to spy on grownups.

Stairs have a funny way of becoming a repository for memories, too. Even less-than-perfect staircases eventually become charming to a homeowner. Maybe it's a banister worn smooth by generations of hands or a creaky step that Mr. Fixit never quite gets around to fixing. And, of course, there's this classic image: that pesky, loose newel cap that caused Jimmy Stewart so much grief (and joy) in the movie *It's a Wonderful Life*. Give a staircase enough time and use, and it will acquire a personality of its own.

Conception

If you're looking at this book, you probably don't need to be told how easy it is to love a beautiful staircase—you know it intuitively. What you might not realize is how wide the world of stairs is. In the last decade or so, the range of options for getting from one floor to the next has exploded. New materials, cutting-edge design, and streamlined manufacturing have made the sky the limit when it comes to stairs. Not only have contemporary designs flourished; the classic designs of years past are more attainable than ever.

In the chapters that follow, you'll find full-color photographs and detailed drawings that show all the options, from classic to contemporary to eclectic. You'll also learn to speak the language of stairs—balustrades, headroom, winders, and so on—so you can work efficiently with architects, designers, builders, and carpenters to bring your staircase ideas to life. In the Repairing and Restoring chapter, you'll find guidance and detailed step-by-step instructions and illustrations for basic repairs and improvements, from installing a runner to adding trim. Whether you're looking for ideas for a major remodel or your dream house—or even if you'd just like to give a plain staircase a new look—this book has something for you.

What: Stairway Anatomy

A Treads

B Riser

C Stringers

D Banister

E Newel posts

F Landings

G Balustrade

H Skirtboards

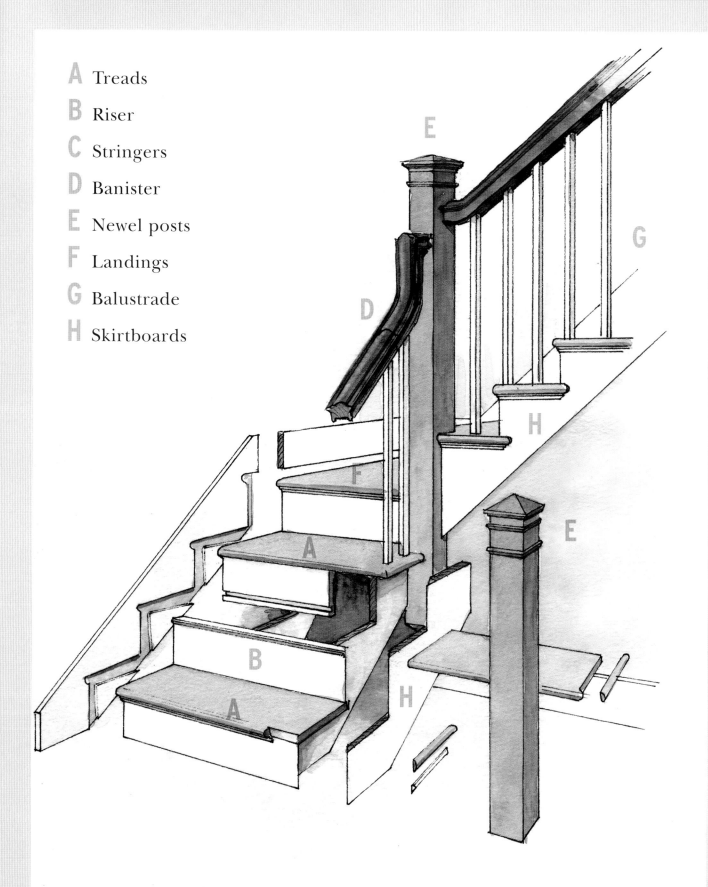

Typical Layouts

L-SHAPED STAIR

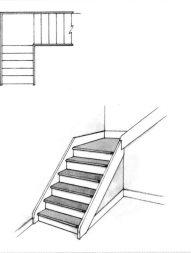

STRAIGHT STAIR WITH OPEN RISERS

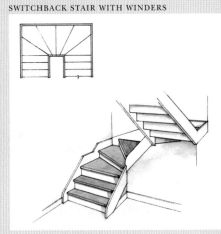

STANDARD SWITCHBACK STAIR

STRAIGHT STAIR

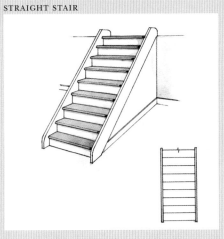

SWITCHBACK STAIR WITH WINDERS

SWITCHBACK STAIR WITH INTERMEDIATE FLIGHT

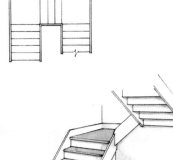

SIDE-FLIGHT STAIR

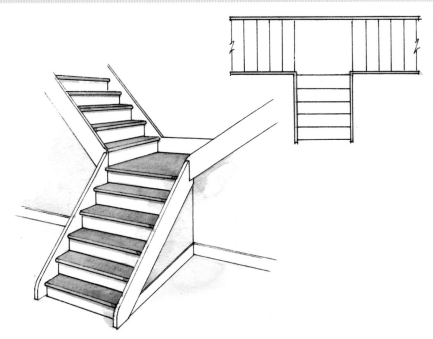

Depending on where they are located in a space, stairs can be freestanding (with no walls on either side) open on one side, or entirely enclosed by walls. As you will see, there are dozens of variations on these common types.

Vocabulary

Knowing just what to call the parts of a staircase—even the stair itself—is tricky. Even carpenters can't agree on terms. The part of the staircase you probably know best—the part you step on—is known as the *tread*. The vertical distance from one tread to the next is normally covered by a board called a *riser*. (Open-riser designs leave this space uncovered.) The relation between the depth of the tread and the height of the riser is among the most critical in stair design, for both comfort and safety.

Treads and risers are generally held in place by parallel boards called *stringers* that run diagonally from one floor to the next. For most stairs, these boards are notched in a saw-tooth pattern to support the treads and risers. The stringers do the important work of keeping stairs straight and stable. They are, however, rarely visible on a finished stair. Instead, the sides are clad with decorative *skirtboards*, often embellished with molding and paneling.

Most people like to hold a rail when they go up or down stairs. Beyond this preference, the law insists that all stairs in houses have a handrail or banister on at least one side. Generally, stairs have a handrail attached to an adjacent wall. Where no wall is present, a handrail is supported by vertical posts called *balusters*. The last and first vertical posts, where the rail ends, are called *newel posts*. On elaborate stairs, the whole handrail assembly is called a *balustrade*.

Stairs that cover long spans or that make one or more turns often feature horizontal spaces called *landings*. Landings allow stairs to turn 90 or 180 degrees and continue up in another direction.

A host of more specialized descriptions is associated with stairs. Consult the glossary on page 174 for more terminology.

Ergonomics

It's important that a staircase fit its users comfortably. But just as the world is full of ill-fitting shirts and too-tight shoes, houses often come with ergonomically challenged stairs. Solutions run from the crude (ever see a bit of foam rubber strategically placed near the bottom of a stair that's a bit short on headroom?) to the unfortunate (bedrooms moved into first-floor living spaces when steep stairs make second-story rooms inaccessible). There is no substitute for a set of stairs designed carefully to provide a lifetime of comfortable use to all the occupants of the house.

Stairs are full of critical dimensions, but three are particularly important. A stair's *rise and run* is essentially the measures of all the treads and risers; this determines how steep the stair is. Building codes limit how much vertical distance (steepness) a stair can cover in a certain horizontal distance, as well as how deep treads must be, so people can comfortably walk on the stairs. If access for people with limited mobility is a concern, take particular care with these dimensions; too steep a rise over too short a run can make a stair dangerous or entirely unusable for an elderly or disabled user (see page 67 for more on accessible stair design).

Headroom is the distance between the beginning of the second floor (the edge of the stair opening) and the steps directly below it. If you've ever banged your head going down an ill-designed stairway, you know why this distance is critical.

It's important that a staircase fit its users comfortably. But just as the world is full of ill-fitting shirts and too-tight shoes, houses often come with ergonomically challenged stairs.

Measurements

Modern building codes were not the first to have a say in the proper use and form of stairs—the Bible weighs in on the subject in Exodus 20:26—but they are probably the most pressing. All codes require stairway access to elevated inhabited spaces.

Here are critical dimensions to keep in mind for any stairway. These conform to most building codes, but when building your own staircase, be sure to check with your local officials before finalizing your plans. These dimensions are also good to bear in mind if you make your own rough sketches to hand over to a pro (see page 15 for an illustration with these parts labeled).

It is imperative to know the specific building codes for your locale. While the measurements noted below generally apply to particular locations, search the Web or contact your local building inspector for building codes pertinent to your area.

THE RULE OF 25

In North America, carpenters who build stairs often speak of "the rule of 25" (or sometimes 24). This is an old rule of thumb for determining tread depth and riser height. The rule is simple: The depth of one tread plus the height of two risers should equal 24 to 25 inches.

United States Acceptable Measurements

Tread depth (run) 10 inches minimum

Riser height (rise) 7 ¾ inches maximum

Stair width 36 inches minimum

Headroom 6 feet, 8 inches minimum

Landing depth 36 inches minimum

Handrail height (above tread) 34–38 inches

Handrail diameter 1 ½–2 inches

Handrail distance from wall
    1 ½ inches minimum

United Kingdom Acceptable Measurements

Tread depth (run) 25.5 cm minimum

Riser height (rise) 20 cm maximum

Stair width 15 cm minimum

Headroom 2 m minimum

Landing depth 1 m minimum

Handrail height (above tread) 0.8–1 m

Handrail diameter 4–5 cm

Handrail distance from wall 4 cm minimum

A STAIRWAY SHOULD FIT ITS SURROUNDINGS, BUT IT MUST ALSO FIT ITS USERS. CURVED AND SPIRAL STAIRCASES MUST BE PLANNED CAREFULLY SO EVERYONE MAY USE THEM.

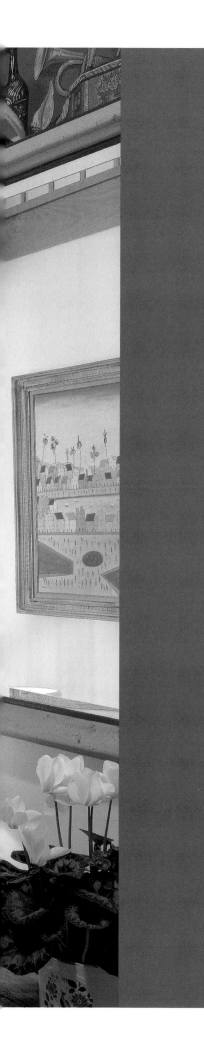

TODAY'S LARGER HOUSES, WITH THEIR OPEN LAYOUTS AND MULTIUSE SPACES, CAN OFTEN BENEFIT FROM A SECOND STAIRCASE THAT PROVIDES ACCESS TO AND FROM COMMONLY USED FAMILY AND ENTERTAINING SPACES.

Traffic Rules

As a general rule, it's a good idea to locate stairs in an area that's convenient to the common areas of a house. Remember, though, stair traffic should flow smoothly and not interfere with other activities. You don't want, for example, a stair to direct traffic into the line of sight of the TV in a family room or, worse still, to send people into the middle of a kitchen work area.

If you're considering a remodel, take the time to make fairly detailed scale drawings of the first and second floors of your home, marking the existing stairs. What works about them in terms of traffic flow? Are they convenient for all family members? Are the stairs convenient to major common spaces? Do they take you out of your way? Maybe the site of the stairway is fine, and remodeling might be only cosmetic. But you might also discover a far better location as you sketch out your floor plans. Show all your ideas to your remodeling contractor. He or she will be able to tell you if the idea is workable.

If you're building from plans, don't take for granted that the stairways are perfectly placed for your needs. Make copies of the plans and sketch in other possible locations. Imagine how you'll use your new rooms and the traffic flow, or the paths you'll walk. Talk to the architect or builder about your ideas.

EIGHTEENTH-CENTURY
CARPENTERS CREATED
BREATHTAKING AND COMPLI-
CATED STAIRCASES FOR
WEALTHY HOMEOWNERS—
ALL WITHOUT MODERN
POWER TOOLS OR MATERIALS.
DESPITE THIS, THE LEVEL
OF CRAFTSMANSHIP AND
DESIGN IN THESE EXAMPLES
IS VERY HIGH.

Multiple Staircases

There's no rule, of course, that limits a house to a single set of stairs between floors. In fact, a grand formal front stair and a small, narrow back stair was a common arrangement in houses in the 1800s.

Sometimes a single staircase simply won't meet all the requirements of a household, particularly a large one. Consider planning for a second stairway that conveniently serves the back rooms of the house.

Of course, some elevated layouts don't need a true staircase at all. Lofts, attics, and other small spaces can be served by a narrow spiral stair or even a fixed ladder. These types of spaces offer a great opportunity to be creative. You'll see inspiring examples of alternative means of ascent in future chapters.

How: Building Stairs

Systems and methods for the construction of stairs in houses have been around since the Renaissance. Architects from Vitruvius to Palladio to Christopher Wren published their thoughts on staircases. A Scot named Peter Nicholson is widely credited with devising, in a book published in the late 1700s, a practical method that made stair construction in homes more scientific system than inspired art—and thus more accessible. Hundreds have attempted to improve on his system since.

Given the sizable body of technical literature devoted to the design of stairs, not to mention the combination of mathematics, art, and received wisdom necessary to construct them, it's amazing to think that they're so common. But carpenters have been building stairs—with or without books—for something like 8,000 years, and they show no signs of stopping now.

MOST OF THE ART AND SCIENCE THAT GOES INTO BUILDING A STAIRCASE REMAINS BEHIND THE SCENES, NEVER REVEALING ITSELF TO THE END USER. CAREFUL LOAD CALCULATIONS AND SPATIAL CONSIDERATIONS GO INTO PLANNING THE FRAMING THAT DETERMINES THE FINISHED SHAPE OF THE STAIR.

Initial Steps

Today, staircases sprout up in houses in several ways. In most new homes and in major remodels, the same contractors who frame and trim the walls, floors, and ceilings also frame and trim the staircase. Plans often do little more than specify the footprint of a stairwell and the type of stair, leaving to the carpenter's (hopefully) considerable skill the finer points of engineering the finished stair. In houses in which an architect or homeowner calls for an elaborate or complicated design, a carpenter specializing in stairs may build the staircase on site, or, in some cases, may take precise measurements on site and then build the staircase framing in a workshop, where he or she can work out complicated angles, curves, and cuts at a workbench instead of at a chaotic jobsite.

If you have a plan—or even just a sketch—of an elaborate stairway, it's worthwhile to talk to a contractor who specializes in stairs. If you're a fervent do-it-yourselfer, you might hire a master stair carpenter to design and frame the staircase and then finish the trim work youself.

Where to find a stair builder? Start in the phone book under—yes, really—

"Stairs." You can also find them in advertisements in homebuilding magazines, and, of course, on the Internet. (See page 174 for more resources.) As for any potential contractor, it's important to check a carpenter's references on past projects and, if at all possible, get at least one reference from a project in process. It may take several weeks for a stair builder to finish a large staircase—including a few days in your home—so you'll want to be sure the contractor is professional, clean, and properly insured.

Whether you plan to build a totally new staircase, order a prefabricated model, or remodel an existing stair, start a folder of interesting designs and inspirational ideas you come across in magazines and books; make notes of what you like and what you think works well. When you meet with your contractor or place your order with the staircase manufacturer, refer to this folder to guide your choices.

Accessible Staircases

As mentioned above, siting a staircase so a person with mobility limitations can use it requires careful consideration. A carpenter

who specializes in stairs may be able to offer suggestions, but it is also a good idea to consult an architect or designer who specializes in accessible home planning. Not only can stairs themselves be made more accessible by careful design, but a variety of devices are available to help people get up stairs with much less difficulty. An architect or designer can help you plan for such a device. Several groups exist that represent these professionals (see Resources, page 174).

STYLE NOTES

You can get a custom look from kit stairs. Many staircase manufacturers sell kits made from unfinished wood components that you can paint or stain to suit your home.

KIT-BUILT STAIRS RANGE
FROM BASIC TO INCREDIBLY
FANCY. THIS UNDERSTATED
SPIRAL IS MADE OF STEEL AND
BLENDS BEAUTIFULLY WITH
ITS SITE. OTHER STEEL STAIR
KITS ARE MADE TO LOOK LIKE
WROUGHT IRON OR WOOD.

Doing It Yourself

Even for the committed do-it-yourselfer, framing staircases is a tricky proposition. Some simple stair designs—such as a single flight from a main floor to a basement, or stairs on a deck or patio—aren't much more difficult than basic framing, and several good framing books are available that can walk you through the process. Precut parts are available at many home centers. Beyond these types of stairs, though, the complexity of the framing and the engineering required to design and build custom staircases increases significantly—and the dangers of an improperly designed and built staircase are considerable.

There is another option. Dozens of companies sell complete precut stair kits for building fairly simple spiral stairs made of steel all the way up to elaborate cantilevered arrangements complete with built-in shelving. Some kit manufacturers work with a space's measurements and provide custom-cut parts. Several large stair manufacturers have websites where you can assemble a virtual stair from their library of components, provide the measurements of your space, and then order the parts, cut to fit—all from your computer. Other manufacturers offer one-size-fits-all kits that allow homeowners to install a staircase with minimal modification of precut parts (see Resources, page 174). In all cases, the complex work of calculating load and cutting parts is done in advance, saving considerable time and effort. And, of course, kit-built stairs are an option for people who don't want to wield a hammer. Most stair manufacturers will install their own kits for free or a nominal charge.

Finally, a do-it-yourselfer can do a great deal to improve a staircase. One of the benefits of big-box home centers is the large selection of prefabricated high-quality staircase parts available right off the rack. Most of these can be installed with standard carpentry tools. Everything from treads to trim can usually be found if you want to repair or improve an existing stair. You can read much more on this in the Repair and Restore chapter.

TWO

CLASSIC STAIRS

From Greek Revival houses to Craftsman bungalows to Federal and Georgian to Queen Anne houses, distinctive stairs occupy an important part of nearly every classic architectural style. Whether straight or curved, steep or gradually inclined, narrow or wide, grand or understated, stairs can make a stylistic statement of their own or be used to tie the whole house together visually.

THE PATINA OF AGE LOOKS
PARTICULARLY GOOD ON
STAIRS. STAIRCASES BEAR
THE MARKS OF THE PEOPLE
WHO USE THEM, AND PARTS
OF THEIR HISTORIES ARE
EMBEDDED IN THOSE MARKS.
DISTINCTIVE IN THEIR SIM-
PLICITY, THESE ARE THE
TIMEWORN STAIRS OF THE
OLSON HOUSE, WHICH WAS
FEATURED IN MANY MID-20TH
CENTURY WORKS BY ANDREW
WYETH, INCLUDING THE
POIGNANT PAINTING
CHRISTINA'S WORLD. THE
ARTIST TRAVERSED THESE
STAIRS FREQUENTLY TO
REACH HIS PAINTING STUDIO
ON AN UPPER FLOOR OF THE
OLD FARM HOUSE, WHICH WAS
BUILT IN THE LATE 1700S.

Right Stairs, Right Place

This chapter presents an overview of stair-case types and examples of classic architectural styles that work well with them. Many modern houses do not adhere strictly to a single architectural style, which means they provide an excellent opportunity to blend favorite elements of one or several styles. There are no hard and fast rules for combining architectural elements—in fact, most architectural styles are variations on or reactions to earlier styles—but it is a good idea to bear in mind the sense of balance and proportion that is at the heart of all good design. Elements of several styles can coexist happily if each is given its proper space and no one element crowds or overshadows another—and as long as they all function well for the people who use the house. Remember also that modern lifestyles aren't always best served by a single formal stair in a foyer. Stairs should be placed in convenient proximity to the places where people spend their time. This may call for investing design energy on neglected back stairs or basement stairs.

IN PRAISE OF OLD STAIRS

"George Washington slept here" is a claim attached to hundreds of houses, great and small, all over the eastern part of the United States. Tourists, the reasoning goes, are bound to be attracted by the prospect of sleeping where a founding father slept. This may be true, but perhaps the proprietors of these inns should advertise that "George Washington climbed these stairs" or "Ben Franklin paused to complete a thought on this landing" or even "Thomas Jefferson slid down this banister." After all, in historic homes, long after the furniture has been carted off to a museum or an auction, the staircase remains. It probably shows a bit of use. The treads may be worn, and perhaps they may even squeak; the banister is probably worn shiny-smooth by the touch of countless hands; maybe a baluster is loose or a newel cap missing. But all of this is a good thing. A stair is a point of contact, more deliberate and intentional than a simple floor or wall. It's easy to imagine a weary guest leaning on a banister as he trudges to a small back bedroom on the second floor, or children spying on parents from behind the balustrade. The wear and tear on an old set of stairs inevitably holds a bit of the history of the people who have occupied the house.

SIMPLICITY AND BALANCE
ARE ALL THE ORNAMENT
THIS STAIRCASE REQUIRES.
MINIMALISM SOUNDS LIKE
A FANCY MODERN DESIGN
TERM, BUT THE ECONOMICAL
USE OF MATERIAL AND
BALANCE IN DESIGN ARE
NOTHING NEW. BY THEM-
SELVES, STRAIGHT, STICKLIKE
BALUSTERS AND A PLAIN
RAILING ARE ORDINARY, BUT
HERE THE COMBINATION IS
INARGUABLY POWERFUL,
ELEGANT, AND GRACEFUL.

Formal Stairs:
THE GRAND ENTRANCE

Sometimes a house just wants to make a statement. Staircases have helped houses (and castles and palaces) make distinctive statements for centuries. You know a distinctive staircase when you stand on one: its generous proportions might make you stand a little taller, and its winding layout may encourage you to take your time and make a grand entrance. Step back, though, and the other hallmark of a formal staircase takes hold. It dominates the space it occupies, and with its curves and well-trimmed surfaces, it is as much a sculpture as a means of transfer from point A to point B.

Typically placed in the center of a large entrance hall or foyer, a grand staircase was once a requirement for well-heeled hosts and hostesses, allowing them to show their wealth and taste and enabling them to greet their guests from a suitable height. The traditional arrangement still works; however, a truly grand staircase is also well suited to the common spaces of many open-plan homes.

Though a single, straight-flight staircase can serve as a formal stair, more commonly, such stairs have a larger footprint; their details and ornaments generally need space. They often have at least one landing and generally have an *L*, switchback, curved, or other multidimensional layout. This not only creates a visually stunning staircase but also makes the stairway into a destination of its own, not just a tilted hallway joining one floor to the next.

Formal doesn't necessarily mean ornate or fancy. Classic Colonial, Federal, and Georgian houses, as well as more contemporary residences, often lend themselves to the restraint and dignity of stairs with simple, neoclassical influences.

The term *neoclassical* may remind us of Greek temples or eighteenth-century Palladian villas, but neoclassicism is more about using classical patterns and proportions than huge slabs of marble (although marble does have a grand history as a material for staircases). A neoclassical style suits an *L*-shaped or switchback layout; where space permits, sweeping curves, and double flight arrangements are not out of the ordinary. Neoclassical details look as appropriate in a Colonial farmhouse as they do in a Federal or Georgian manor. The important

thing is the balance of details. Gracefully turned balusters, a carved, curving banister, a distinct newel post, and carefully trimmed treads and skirtboards are all hallmarks of this style. Rather than any single detail dominating, many small details balance one another perfectly.

Restraint and subtlety are all well and good, but sometimes a statement should be made nice and clear and an entrance shown off with just a bit of fanfare. Those with adventurous tastes—like the Victorians—have had something to say about formal stairs.

STYLE NOTES

When a staircase is large, dominating one or two walls and parts of two floors, consider how other details of the surrounding space interact with this massive central feature. It's often effective to tie the stairway to the adjoining halls or rooms with continuous details. For example, staircase skirtboards can match or complement the baseboard molding in the rest of the room. Another striking touch on a half-enclosed stair is wainscoting that continues up the wall side of the stairs, matching the height of the banister with the top of wainscoting for an effect called a *shadow railing*.

Asymetric Elegance

The plans of Victorian Gothic, Italian Revival, and Queen Anne houses generally aren't symmetric, which allows for more freedom in siting a front staircase. In Victorian houses, stairs can be placed quite naturally to one side of a front entryway, perhaps adjacent to a living room or library.

This freedom extends to detailing as well. Victorian stairs tend to be heavy in their proportions and ornamentation, featuring elaborately carved and turned balustrades inspired by Gothic, Asian, and neoclassical patterns. Instead of a regular arrangement of slender, round balusters, Victorian balustrades might feature square-profiled balusters or balusters combined with raised panels—or the balustrade might simply employ a single, elaborately carved or forged panel in lieu of balusters. Newels tend to be large, square, and heavily decorated in any of dozens of styles. Victorian style is the original eclecticism, and a Victorian-style formal staircase should reflect this. After all, the real Victorians thought nothing of placing two-foot-tall carved lions, each holding an early electric lamp, on top of newels.

THE STAIRCASE ISN'T LARGE, BUT EXQUISITE DETAILS ABOUND IN THIS ITALIANATE SWITCHBACK. THE BALUSTRADE HAS THREE BALUSTER DESIGNS AND AN EXQUISITELY CARVED NEWEL PERCHED ON A CURVED STARTING STEP. PARTICULARLY STRIKING ARE THE UNDERSIDES OF THE STRINGERS FOR THE SECOND FLIGHT OF STAIRS, WHICH ARE TYPICALLY FINISHED FLAT BUT HERE ARE CUT SAW-TOOTHED AND TRIMMED AND FINISHED TO MATCH THE TOP SIDE, GIVING THE IMPRESSION THAT THEY ARE FLOATING.

THIS STAIRCASE, OFTEN
CALLED A SIDE-FLIGHT
STAIR, WAS POPULAR ON LUX-
URY OCEAN LINERS AND IN
LARGE HOMES. TWO FLIGHTS
OF STAIRS BRANCH OFF AT
RIGHT ANGLES FROM A
SINGLE LANDING. THE NEED
TO BE ECONOMICAL WITH
SPACE AND THE DESIRE TO
FACILITATE A GRACEFUL
ENTRANCE GAVE BIRTH TO
THIS ELEGANT DESIGN.

FIRST IMPRESSIONS

Ergonomics are a priority for modern stairs, but this wasn't always true. Sometimes a first impression was more important than comfort. The Alexander Ramsey House in St. Paul, Minnesota, was the grandest home in the state when it was completed in 1872, and it featured all the latest in European architecture and design fashions (Mrs. Ramsey had just returned from a trip to Europe with two boxcars full of furniture and art). The black walnut staircase is one of the first and finest details one notices on entering the three-story Second Empire mansion. It seems no expense was spared, no convenience overlooked. But when climbing the stairs, modern visitors are frequently struck by something odd. The graceful balustrade is placed distinctly—and uncomfortably—low. It is not, as some guess, because people were shorter back then. The odd proportions of this Victorian staircase were meant to give the house the appearance of having very high ceilings, and, even more important, encouraged Victorian ladies to descend the staircase gracefully, without any unsightly support from the railing.

CAST IRON, WHICH CAN EXPRESS MYRIAD ORNATE DESIGNS, IS AN EXCELLENT ALTERNATIVE TO WOOD FOR VICTORIAN-STYLE BANISTERS AND BALUSTRADES.

Casual Stairs

STYLE NOTES

Victorian style is more than dark wood and heavy carving. Color is a natural addition to a formal Victorian stair. Consider a colored carpet runner for the stairs or colorful tile or paper for the walls. An arched window with a pane of stained glass is a crowning touch for the landing on a formal Victorian stair.

Not every staircase lives in a front hall of course, and not every house needs a formal, showcase stairway. Modern lifestyles often revolve around a kitchen or a family room, which are more casual, comfortable spaces, and access to the second floor should suit this style.

Of course, this isn't really new. Staircases in classic vernacular styles—farmhouses, cottages, and cabins, to name a few—often ran beside a central chimney and so conveniently terminated near a house's central gathering space: the fireplace hearth. Consider following their example if you're planning a major remodel or even building a new home. There's nothing wrong with a formal front-hall staircase, but there's a lot to be said for putting the staircase where it's easily accessible from the major activity centers of a house. A casual approach to staircases needn't be less beautiful; it just has different priorities.

Comfort and Convenience

The Arts and Crafts style is a particularly good example of an informal, comfortable approach to house design. It was conceived of and still is an excellent alternative to the formality of the Victorian and neoclassical styles. Rather than make a statement with grand spaces, the Arts and Crafts style emphasizes the creation of sheltering spaces.

Arts and Crafts houses tend to be lower, more earthbound structures than their soaring neoclassical or Victorian neighbors. The rooms are often smaller and more compartmentalized, giving a cozier, more private feeling. With respect to interior design layout and details, the emphasis is on sheltering spaces that center on the comfort of the family rather than on the entertainment of guests. Stairs continue this theme. Rarely does a staircase in a bungalow or an Arts and Crafts cottage rise more than half a flight without a generous landing. Much more common is an *L*-shaped layout with a very short first flight. Stairs situated front and center in an entryway are uncommon. Instead, stairs tend to hug a side wall, providing easy access but not overwhelming the front hall. The distance from one floor to the next in a bungalow isn't necessarily any less than in any other house, but the stairs, by dividing flights into human-size portions, make the distance seem more attainable and the stairway more inviting. Ornamentation in Arts and Crafts homes is influenced more by medieval Gothic or Eastern motifs than by neoclassical. On staircases, newels tend toward boxy, substantial forms with pyramid or spherical caps.

THE BACK STAIRS

If you had the luxury of building a home for yourself in the nineteenth century, it was almost a forgone conclusion that you would have an elaborate formal staircase in the front entry. For many wealthy home-owners, this led to at least one immediate dilemma: How would the hired help get upstairs?

Most houses solved this problem with an additional narrow, steep, sometimes spi-raling stairway hidden in the back of the house. Servants could thus move incon-spicuously between floors—but as a matter of course, these stairs were useful to all members of the household. A gentleman's business associates might join him quietly in his study for a discreet cigar without disturbing his wife and her friends in the parlor. Or a son or daughter, returning home after curfew, might try his or her luck with the back stairs. The utility of the back stair—or any second stairway—is as apparent now as it was then. If a floor plan will allow it, a second stairway is always a good idea.

THIS SIMPLE *L*-SHAPED STAIR-CASE IS SUBTLE IN DETAIL BUT RICH IN CRAFTSMANSHIP. THE MASSIVE NEWEL POSTS ARE DECORATED WITH A SIM-PLE ARTS AND CRAFTS DESIGN THAT EMPHASIZES THE BEAUTY OF THE WOOD AND ECHOES THE STRONG GEO-METRIC FORMS COMMON TO THE STYLE.

IT'S A SMALL STAIRCASE, BUT IN TYPICAL CRAFTSMAN STYLE, IT INTEGRATES SEAMLESSLY WITH THE REST OF THE HOUSE. THE LONG SECOND FLIGHT CONTINUES BEHIND THE PARTITION. THE SLATS ON THE TOP OF THE PARTITION AND THE NARROW CASEMENT AT THE LANDING ARE SIMPLE TOUCHES, BUT THEY MAKE THIS OTHERWISE DARK STAIR LIGHT AND INVITING.

STYLE NOTES

Whichever style of stairs you choose, it's a good idea to have an Arts and Crafts mindset with respect to the space underneath. A staircase remodel is a good opportunity to consider building something useful into this often underused space. Anything from a bookshelf to a powder room can find a home under a staircase.

Quality Materials

Traditionally turned balusters are common, but just as frequently, a bungalow balustrade features unadorned, slat-like balusters of beautifully grained oak or mahogany. Often, the craftsmanship used to join raw materials becomes an ornament itself, as if often seen in the exposed tenons and pegs of Craftsman-style furniture. In general, Arts and Crafts designs tend to be warm and welcoming, well scaled for everyday life.

Wood finishes on stairs in particular seem to embody the spirit of this style. The wood itself is rarely heavily carved and is always shown to its best advantage, both visual and tactile. The combined effect makes the material seem alive, welcoming, and practically begging to be touched. All this helps explain why staircases built in the Arts and Crafts style seem to invite people to linger or even to sit down.

People often sum up the Arts and Crafts design philosophy with a quote from the movement's founder, William Morris: "Have nothing in your house that you do not know to be useful, or believe to be beautiful."

Secondary Uses

This describes another hallmark of well-thought-out casual staircases—the stairs as a seating area. A truly well-situated and inviting set of stairs can quickly make itself useful as a casual seating area. Such a stair adjoins, but doesn't divide or dominate, an active living space, such as a front hall or a family room or even an open-plan kitchen. It's wide at the bottom, often flaring or including extra starting steps. Finally, its surfaces, instead of being heavily decorated, are simple but attractive, warm in feeling, and not overly delicate.

Staircases that fit this description appear in houses of every style, but ranches and split-levels—architectural styles rarely associated with staircases—are particularly suited to these casual stairs. Ranches, both new and old, typically have a family room or entertainment space served by a wide flight of only a few stairs. It's little wonder, then, that people tend to congregate on these stairs.

THIS STAIRCASE IS A CONTEMPORARY ADAPTATION OF THE ARTS AND CRAFTS NOTION OF UNASSUMING BEAUTY AND SUBTLE UTILITY. IT IS SITUATED FOR CONVENIENCE TO THE FRONT DOOR BUT DOESN'T OVERWHELM THE ENTRY SPACE. THE DOUBLE-WIDTH FIRST FLIGHT, WITH ITS WARM-TONED WOODEN TREADS, MAKES THE STAIRCASE BOTH PASSAGEWAY AND SEATING SPACE. THE SECOND LANDING TAKES THIS IDEA FURTHER WITH A BUILT-IN SETTLE SITUATED UNDER THE BUMP-OUT WINDOW.

DEDICATED
STAIRWAY SEATING

Some stairs go so far as to incorporate
actual dedicated seating into the design,
emphasizing the staircase as not a mere
passageway but an actual destination.
A common expression of the twin Arts
and Crafts ideals of beauty and utility is
built-in furniture or cabinetry, especially in
stairs. In the turn-of-the-twentieth-century
designs of Gustav Stickley and Charles and
Henry Greene, a settle often adjoins the
foot of a staircase.

A SETTLE AT THE FOOT OF A
STAIRCASE—ESPECIALLY IN AN
ENTRY HALL—WAS A CON-
STANT FEATURE OF PERIOD
CRAFTSMAN DESIGNS BY
GUSTAV STICKLEY AND THE
GREENE AND GREENE ARCHI-
TECTURAL FIRM. IT ALSO
EMBODIES THE SPIRIT OF A
TRULY FINE CASUAL STAIR.
IT'S INVITING, WARM, AND
SCALED TO HUMAN PROPOR-
TIONS RATHER THAN BEING
OVERTLY IMPRESSIVE.

THREE

CONTEMPORARY STAIRS

OPEN RISERS AND GLASS PANELS INSTEAD OF INDIVIDUAL BALUSTERS ARE TYPICAL OF THE SLEEK AESTHETICS OF MODERN ARCHITECTURE. A HUGE PICTURE WINDOW—ANOTHER MODERNIST FAVORITE—MAKES A STUNNING BACKDROP FOR THIS SLEEK SWITCHBACK.

For most of the history of residential staircases, it was unthinkable to make a staircase of any material other than wood or brick or—for the very wealthy—stone. Cast iron played a supporting role in balustrades, but the heavy work of steps was accomplished almost exclusively by wood and occasionally by cut stone or brick.

Form Follows Material

Construction materials have changed dramatically in the past seventy-five years. In general, materials and manufacturing processes have improved and become vastly more accessible. As technology and industry have improved, art and design have been quick to follow. Architects and designers have embraced new materials and new techniques, taking it upon themselves to find thousands of new uses for materials. Add to this the fact that more people than ever own houses—and not only own them, but continually improve them as never before—and you have the perfect conditions for unparalleled innovation and growth in residential architecture.

Specifically, this means the staircase. Never a shrinking violet to begin with, it has been pushed, pulled, twisted, and spiraled into forms unimaginable only a century ago. Staircases retain their showcase status, but with the advent of lighter, stronger materials, architects and builders are also able to build staircases that are truly functional sculpture—stairs that practically disappear into a room or take up astonishingly little floor space.

Of course, it's not all aluminum and glass. Woodworkers have kept pace, and there are craftspeople working today who have lost none of their predecessors' skill with wood but have benefited from contemporary advances in tools, materials, and design. This is a golden age for all aspects of home construction.

In this chapter, you'll get a sense of the state of the art, so to speak, of residential stairs. Replicating nontraditional designs in your own home will require the assistance of an open-minded architect and contractor, but once you've found them, the sky is the limit.

Reimagining the Traditional

Despite the prediction of many notable modern architects some fifty years ago, most people live in houses that bear more than a little resemblance to the homes their great-grandparents grew up in. Of course there have been innovations, renovations, and even revolutions (think of the single-story suburban ranch, a design largely unimaginable to someone growing up in the nineteenth century), but we still expect a house to provide the same sense of shelter and separation from the outside world they always have.

This is also true of staircases. They're still here, of course; they have not been supplanted by elevators or some still unimagined way of getting from one floor to the next. The distinctions between formal and casual are less sharp than in the past, but not less important. In contemporary-style homes, staircases sometimes appear front and center, curving and twisting to fulfill a mission to impress and

inspire, just as they did in an antebellum plantation. In the same way, we find stairs that embrace the family centers of a home, efficiently and attractively moving traffic between floors in a way that would be entirely recognizable to the most fervent partisan of the Arts and Crafts movement. In cutting-edge contemporary homes, we also find a growing third class of stairs. Small-scale stairs are becoming increasingly common—think of the humble split-level ranch or of the many contemporary designs that incorporate lofts or other elevated living spaces. The flexibility of modern construction makes the range of multilevel areas accessible.

Freestanding Open Stairs

Staircases that extend from one floor to the next with external support in between are nothing new, as the previous chapter shows. People have always gravitated toward stair designs that give the impression of floating or weightlessness—functional sculptures for the front hall. What's new is how accessible these functional sculptures are and the variety of ways they can now be executed.

STYLE NOTES

Glass block is a readily available and attractive material for all sorts of contemporary staircase applications. It's ideal for exterior walls adjoining stairs. More affordable than a wall-size window, glass block allows light in but preserves a measure of privacy. It's also possible to build dramatic curved walls with glass block.

GREEN TREADS

Many modern materials reflect growing concerns about the consumption of natural resources. Staircase parts are no exception. Rather than use wood from slow growing hardwood species, consider sustainable woods, such as bamboo, for treads and risers.

Another green option is treads made from recycled tires and bottles, which are available in attractive colors and finishes.

OPEN RISERS MAKE A LIGHT, GRACEFUL STATEMENT IN A LIGHT-FILLED OPEN-PLAN HOME. WOOD AND STEEL SUP-PORTS WORK TOGETHER TO CREATE THIS CONTEMPORARY *L*-SHAPED STAIRCASE. NOTICE HOW THE PATTERN OF THE RAILING MIRRORS THE PAT-TERN CREATED BY THE EDGES OF THE TREADS.

PANELS OF TEMPERED GLASS
TAKE THE PLACE OF INDIVID-
UAL BALUSTRADES ON THIS
FLOATING STAIR. THE COMBI-
NATION OF METAL, GLASS,
AND CONCRETE IS EFFECTIVE
AND EYE-CATCHING.

REPURPOSED STAIRS

Another thoroughly contemporary approach to stairs involves looking outside the house for design inspiration—and sometimes for the stairs themselves. Whole companies exist to serve the unique staircase needs of every type of structure, from factories to submarines to fire escapes to luxury yachts.

Some of the designs are quite ingenious; highly efficient alternating tread designs, for example, are quite common for factory stairs. If your tastes run in this direction, spend some time on the Internet searching for "industrial stairs," and you'll get some intriguing and potentially inspiring results.

Stairs as Sculpture

From prefabricated steel stair kits to poured concrete to handcrafted wooden stairs reinforced with the latest in engineered support beams, relatively inexpensive and widely available materials and expertise have pushed the limits of unsupported spans in residential buildings.

Steel, iron, and aluminum are present in homes like never before—and not just in spaces where the predominant style can be summed up with the word *industrial.* Prefabricated or custom-crafted metalwork is an ideal material for all aspects of residential stairs. For balustrades and decorative ele-

ments, artisans working in iron and steel create a huge array of this functional sculpture in styles suited to almost every aesthetic. As a structural material, metal is malleable and at the same time strong in a way that wood cannot be, allowing for a wide variety of shapes and layouts.

Stairs needn't be made entirely of metal to utilize metal's advantages. A metal structure can be an ideal framework for wood, glass, stone, or concrete. In many staircases, metal is combined with wood and glass in order to reap the unique advantages of all three materials.

Other materials are now available to create weightless effects in stairs. One of the less heralded advances of the twentieth century is the wide availability of glass— and not just for windows. Not only is glass affordable, it also can be fabricated to carry tremendous loads such that it is now a practical option for balustrades, treads, and even entire staircases. Judiciously applied, glass can effectively banish all traces of the dark, claustrophobic stairwell. Traversing this kind of stair is like walking on air.

SOME STAIRS SEEM TO INVITE YOU TO THE FIRST STEP; THIS ONE LITERALLY GIVES YOU A HAND UP. A STEEL I-BEAM MAKES FOR A SOLID SINGLE STRINGER ON THIS WHIMSICAL, MODERN LOFT STAIR.

Custom-poured concrete has become the darling of architects for creating durable, beautiful flooring and countertops. It is also an ideal material for stairs because it allows designers and builders unsurpassed freedom to build complex curved forms. Concrete can be used in very traditional staircase forms; its tremendous versatility allows for organic, flowing shapes that are virtually impossible to create in other materials.

In addition to versatility of form, poured concrete is remarkable for the wide variety of ways it can be finished. Customers are demanding beauty as well as durability from poured structures, and, as a result, artisans and professional contractors have developed techniques that make concrete resemble anything from rustic, weathered adobe to gleaming, polished marble—and just about everything in between. And the finishes are very durable and low maintenance—perfect for staircases.

Concrete also lends itself to combination with other materials such as metal, glass, and tile. Balustrades and railings can be integrated into the stairs when the forms are poured for a seamless effect. Glass block or tile can be added on to the concrete. The possibilities are nearly limitless.

CUSTOM-POURED CONCRETE ALLOWS UNSURPASSED FREEDOM TO CREATE COMPLICATED CURVED FORMS. HERE, THE STAIRS SEEM MORE LIQUID THAN SOLID AS THEY FLOW FROM ONE FLOOR TO THE NEXT.

Stone is one of the ultimate luxuries in staircase construction, as it has been for centuries. It is just as suitable for contemporary tastes as it is for more classical ones. Marble is, of course, a timeless choice, but gorgeous contemporary staircases can be built from soapstone, limestone, granite, and many other types of stone.

Carved stone offers the greatest flexibility for custom stairs, but it is quite expensive. It is possible to get much of the stunning effect of stone in a remodeled staircase by having treads fabricated from a classic, durable stone, such as slate.

Stone is more readily available and easier to work with than ever. Designers are expanding notions of what is possible with stone by combining it with metal and glass to make gravity-defying modern staircases.

Stone needn't be a budget-busting luxury, though. The variety of stone available as prefabricated tiles, fortunately, is quite considerable, making stone a much more accessible choice than it once was.

STONE IS ONE OF THE ULTIMATE LUXURIES IN STAIRCASE CONSTRUCTION—AND IT'S JUST AS SUITABLE FOR CONTEMPORARY TASTES AS IT IS FOR CLASSICAL. CUSTOM-FLARED STEPS FOLLOW THE CURVES OF THE WALLS IN THIS STRIKING ENCLOSED STAIR.

FOUR

ALTERNATIVES TO STAIRCASES

Traditional staircases, with their sturdy framing and wide walkways, are hard to beat as a passage from one large living space to another. They're efficient and accessible, not to mention attractive. But staircases do have their limitations. For one, no matter how carefully designed or sited, a full-fledged stair-case takes up a considerable amount of space. This can make the traditional approach impractical or impossible for projects such as converting an attic to a living space. What's more, some elevated spaces have potential use as living or storage space but don't need standard stairs.

TRADITIONAL STAIRCASES AREN'T THE ONLY WAY UP. SOMETIMES, MORE MODEST DEVICES ARE JUST THE TICKET. A LADDER—EVEN A MODEST FOLD-UP LADDER LIKE THIS ONE—LENDS AN AIR OF SECRECY AND WONDER TO A HIGH SPACE. LADDERS ARE PERFECT FOR PROVIDING ACCESS TO COZY, OUT-OF-THE-WAY ATTICS AND LOFTS.

Other Means of Ascent

Fortunately, there are alternatives to traditionally framed staircases. As people begin to consider more creative and efficient ways to use otherwise neglected space in their houses, they begin to consider alternatives to traditional stairs—everything from prefabricated spiral stairs to retractable attic stairs to, yes, rope ladders.

This chapter presents some of these viable and flexible alternatives to traditional stairs. Be careful, though—after seeing these, you're bound to think differently about any unused high spaces in your home.

Spiral Stairs

Spiral stairs work a lot like regular stairs—they're accessible to most people, and it's not too difficult to move small pieces of furniture up and down them—but they have one significant advantage—a small footprint. Spiral stairs are little more than trapezoidal treads and a railing winding around a central post, so they can easily occupy as few as 10 square feet (1 sq m) of floor space. Most spiral stairs are open-tread designs, and spirals made of metal can be built of very slender components, allowing them to be visually inconspicuous. All this makes them perfect for providing access to a floor above without making a big impact below.

Lofted bedrooms, converted attics, and other spaces that don't serve a large number of people at once are all excellent candidates for spiral-stair access.

Spiral stairs needn't be inconspicuous —in fact, for many, they have an undeniable aesthetic appeal. Fine classic examples include the massive spiral stairs of nineteenth-century Shaker meeting houses (these giant helixes were often built in pairs). Today, spiral stairs are manufactured in hundreds of styles from dozens of materials. Basic steel or aluminum spiral stair kits can be purchased for less than $1,000 (see Resources, page 174) and set up by a homeowner or technicians in a matter of hours. These sorts of spirals are ideal for quickly adding convenient access to converted attic or garage space. At the other extreme, custom-crafted spirals, handmade from hardwood using traditional joinery, can be as much a showcase for a carpenter's skill as a piece of fine furniture—with all the attendant costs. Whether the style of the house is minimalist industrial or extroverted Second Empire, a spiral design exists to complement it.

THE STAIRS OF GENIUS

The notion of a private sanctuary accessible only by a narrow, hidden stairway is romantic and mysterious, but it's hardly new. In fact, it has some very famous precedents. In the Santissima Annunziata monastery in Milan, Italy, researchers discovered a hidden switchback staircase that led to several secret rooms that belonged, five centuries earlier, to none other than Leonardo da Vinci. It's possible that he painted the *Mona Lisa* in one of these secret workshops.

CONSTRUCTED OF HEAVILY
ORNAMENTED STEEL AND
BRASS, THIS SPIRAL STAIRCASE
HAS ALL THE CHARM OF
ANTIQUE VICTORIAN
WROUGHT IRON FOR A FRAC-
TION OF THE COST, BEING
BUILT FROM A PREFABRICATED
KIT. THE SITE IS IDEAL FOR
A SPIRAL. IT PROVIDES CON-
VENIENT ACCESS FROM A
TWO-STORY GREAT ROOM
TO BEDROOMS ON THE
UPPER FLOOR.

Raising a Spiral

Spirals can be installed in a couple of ways. They can rise to a stairwell opening in an otherwise complete ceiling—that is, the stair goes up toward an opening only slightly larger than the stair's footprint, just as a traditional staircase does. The opening is generally three-quarters of a circle or a square, with the last quarter providing the landing. More commonly, spirals provide access to an elevated space that is not entirely closed off from the rooms below—a loft, for instance. In these arrangements, a spiral requires no stairwell opening, as its landing is simply the edge of the upper floor.

Keep in mind that the space savings of a very small spiral (one with narrow treads) comes at the expense of ease of use. A wider spiral not only is easier to ascend and descend but also makes transporting things safer and easier. Laying out the angle and rise of a spiral stair isn't any simpler than for a standard staircase; factors like headroom and steepness still come into play. When in doubt, it's worthwhile to have an experienced professional do the work.

PART STAIR, PART LADDER, THIS INDUSTRIAL ALTERNATING-TREAD STAIRWAY IS A PERFECT FIT WITH THE HIGH CEILINGS AND BRICK WALLS OF A URBAN LOFT. STEEL CABLES AND TURN-BUCKLES CONTINUE THE INDUSTRIAL THEME WITHOUT ADDING TOO MUCH VISUAL WEIGHT.

Ladders

Ladders are the grandfathers of staircases and have a proud history of accessing everything from leaf-filled gutters to haylofts to heavily fortified castle walls (some of the most sophisticated ancient ladders were conceived as siege engines). In today's houses, ladders continue to provide utilitarian access to attics and high bookshelves. They are also been pressed into service for modernist mini-lofts and other private nooks to which easy access isn't necessary—or necessarily desirable.

Ladders create a sense of mystery and privacy, and there's no shortage of real and metaphorical ladders in poetry and stories; for example, Dante imagines a ladder of love leading to heaven in his *Divine Comedy*. Perhaps that's why they're perfect for helping create a personal hiding place, whether a distraction-free meditation space in an attic or a painting room tucked up in the roof of a garage.

Ladders can be as a simple or as complicated as space and taste dictate. Some lofts require little more than a wide wooden ladder; other tastes are suited by industrial ironwork contraptions that would look quite at home on a battleship.

WHEN LADDERS ARE AN
OPTION, A WORLD OF POSSI-
BILITIES OPENS FOR THE CRE-
ATIVE USE OF SPACE. THE TOP
OF THIS MASSIVE BUILT-IN
ENTERTAINMENT AND STOR-
AGE UNIT WOULD HAVE BEEN
LITTLE MORE THAN A HOME
FOR DUST. WITH A SIMPLE
LADDER, THE SPACE IS TRANS-
FORMED INTO A USEFUL
LOFTED OFFICE.

STYLE NOTES

Stairs and ladders are two-way streets;
perhaps the ultimate expression of
daring in inter-floor transit is the
decidedly one-way fire pole. A 10-foot
(3 m) drop probably isn't everyone's
cup of tea, but if a loft or second-floor
space has a more prosaic way down, a
beautiful brass fire pole might be the
ultimate indulgence.

Ladders Built to Code

Ladders usually aren't carefully governed
by residential building codes (although
they may be prohibited by code for "living
spaces"), but commonsense guidelines per-
tain. For most uses, it's important to secure
ladders at least to the upper space.
Ladders should have a comfortable slope,
like a staircase—1 foot (30.5 cm) of run
for every 4 feet (1.25 m) of vertical rise is a
good rule of thumb. It's also a good idea
to provide a handhold beyond the landing,
either by extending the ladder 3 feet (1 m)
beyond the landing or by adding a railing.

Retractable attic ladders are probably
the most common ladders found in houses.
Generally, they provide convenient access
to storage space, but there's no reason
why they can't provide access to more
frequently used spaces as well. Hardware
stores and home centers sell several sizes of
ladder to fit most attic openings. These are
generally made of wood and fold or slide
down when a handle on the attic door is
pulled. Lighter and more visually appealing
accordion-style ladders are another option.

A SIMPLE WOODEN LADDER
WITH A RAILING LEADS FROM
THE MAIN STAIRCASE LAND-
ING INTO A THIRD-STORY
LOFT. THE LADDER CAN BE
PULLED OUT OF THE WAY
WHEN NOT IN USE AND THE
OPENING COVERED WITH A
MATCHING PANEL.

RESIDENTIAL ELEVATORS

The layout of some stairs makes a stair lift undesirable or impossible; for example, the stairs may have several landings that keep the rails from running straight to the top. In this situation, a residential elevator may be a viable alternative. An elevator takes up less space than you might imagine (in fact, many newer homes are designed with stacked closets so residential elevators can be added easily). They can often be built into a closet or other out-of-the-way space on the first floor and rise into a second-floor bedroom. However, they are expensive and require professional installation.

SEVERAL COMPANIES MANU-
FACTURE STAIRCASE LIFTS
THAT RETROFIT EASILY TO
EXISTING STAIRCASES, ALLOW-
ING ALL MEMBERS OF THE
HOUSEHOLD EASY ACCESS TO
UPPER FLOORS.

Accessible Alternatives

Spirals and ladders are alternatives for spaces where staircases are impractical or undesirable, but what about when staircases are unusable? Traditional stairs can be a significant barrier for people with physical disabilities or limited mobility. Fortunately, stairs can be modified to make the whole house accessible to all.

Exterior Ramps

For exterior stairs, ramps are a good alternative. They can be built custom into decks, or prefabricated metal ramps can be purchased to suit the entryway. Another option is to install a lift beside the front stairs. This is a good solution where space is tight. The Resources chapter (see page 174) has additional information on purchasing accessible stairs.

Interior Lifts

Interior stairs are another challenge. Many disabled or older homeowners are forced to reconfigure their houses or even move because an upstairs bedroom is no longer comfortably accessible. One solution is to install a motorized lift that runs on rails that follow the path of the staircase. Several companies make such devices (see Resources, page 174) for new staircases and for retrofit installation on existing stairs. These require only the addition of rails and the lift. The lift folds away when not in use, and the rails can be integrated to such a degree that they are hardly noticeable.

SOMETIMES THE DETAILS MAKE THE DIFFERENCE. FROM THE CASCADE OF STARTING STEPS TO THE FINIALS ON THE NEWEL TO THE CAN-TILEVERED THIRD FLIGHT, ALL THE LITTLE TOUCHES HARMONIZE PERFECTLY ON THIS MAJESTIC GEORGIAN SWITCHBACK.

FIVE

DETAILS

Whether you're planning a staircase for a new house or con-templating remodeling an existing set of stairs, eventually you'll get down to details—and staircases have their share of details. From balusters to nosing to lighting, attention to detail can make a staircase in any style extraordinary.

In this chapter, you'll find a catalog of clever touches and accents. Not every detail in a staircase needs to scream for attention; you can pick just a few favorite touches and still make a big difference. If you're remodeling a stair, many staircase details are easily adaptable to existing construction. Whatever your project, start with the treads and work up.

Skirtboards

On most traditional stairs, the stringers that carry the actual load are covered by decorative boards called *skirtboards*. These are often trimmed or carved for decorative effect, but they also serve the practical purpose of protecting the more delicate drywall or plaster of the walls. For a clean, continuous effect, continue the baseboard molding from the rest of room up the stairs. Skirtboards don't have to be boards;

metal and ceramic tile are excellent alternatives that can bring texture and color to a staircase and protect its walls from dings.

THE OVERALL EFFECT OF THIS STAIRCASE IS IMPRESSIVE, WITH ITS MULTIPLE CANTILEVERS AND APPROACHES, BUT DON'T OVERLOOK THE SMALL DETAILS, SUCH AS THE WAY THE NOSING WRAPS ALL THE WAY AROUND THE STAIR, THE WAY THE CARVING ON THE SKIRTBOARDS REINFORCES THE SENSATION THAT THE STAIRS ARE FLOATING, AND THE WAY THE DENTIL AND PILASTER SHADOW RAILING ECHO THE BANISTER.

Embellishments

Carpet runners are another easy way to add color and pattern, especially to a set of wooden stairs. Runners must be secured to treads to avoid a tripping hazard. Fortunately, there is an astonishing variety of decorative brass and nickel-plated rods that keep runners in place stylishly.

DUST CORNERS ARE A QUIN-TESSENTIALLY VICTORIAN DETAIL, AND FOR ANY STAIR-CASE, THEY'RE A GREAT WAY TO ADD A WHIMSICAL DECO-RATIVE TOUCH FOR LITTLE MONEY AND EFFORT.

DUST CORNERS

The Victorians seem to have thought of everything when it comes to trimming out a staircase, but dust corners have to be their crowning achievement. Born of necessity (middle-class Victorian house-wives had few servants) but finished with typical flair, dust corners are small, polished brass triangles that fit into the back corners of steps—the hardest part to sweep clean. Even in an age of vacu-ums with crevice attachments, it's hard to deny their appeal, and they're a perfect touch for a Victorian house. Reproduction dust corners are available from retailers specializing in restoration (see Resources, page 174).

Balustrades

Balustrades are often the most strongly decorative element of the staircase, classic or modern, so attention to detail in this area can pay the biggest dividends in remodeling a stairway. A balustrade can define the style for the staircase and the surrounding space. It is well worth your attention.

BALUSTRADES ARE FULL OF OPPORTUNITIES FOR CREATIVE EXPRESSION AND EVEN FOR DISPLAY. IN THIS LIGHT WOOD STAIR, CARPENTERS BUILT IN CUSTOM FRAMES FOR ASIAN-MOTIF CERAMIC WALL TILES. THE FRAMES CAST MAGNIFICENT SHADOWS WHEN LIGHT FROM THE GENEROUS WINDOWS STRIKES THEM.

Railings

Railings are an unusual decorative element in that they have both visual and tactile elements; they are that rare decoration that you routinely touch and even lean on. A good railing is beautiful to see and touch and is strong enough to lean on and resist the occasional knock.

Over the Post

There are, broadly speaking, three common ways to install a railing. A railing can run continuously from top to bottom over balusters and newels—a style that carpenters call *over the post*. This style is far and away the most common treatment for curved stairs of all sorts, but especially in neoclassical styles (and on many spirals). At landings, the carpenter typically makes the transition from diagonal to horizontal with an abrupt curve called a *gooseneck*. At the top and bottom newels, the railing finishes with a graceful outward curve called a *volute* (the balusters typically follow this curve, forming a semicircle around the newel).

There's something undeniably beguiling about a sinuous ribbon of hardwood winding weightlessly down the stairs. Wood is an obvious and excellent choice for such a railing, not only because it finishes beautifully but also because it is warm and smooth to the touch. You may also want to choose wood just to witness the craftsmanship that goes into bending straight hardwood boards into effortless curves. Such a rail is itself a work of art and considerable engineering. Rarely are these sorts of railings simple dowels; more often, they are machined to a profile pleasing to both the eye and hand. Wrought iron also found its way onto many neoclassical stairs as railings, especially those with intricately worked-iron balusters. On more modern stairs, however, metal and even clear polycarbonate take curves readily and are visually attractive.

THIS STAIRWAY IS A STUDY IN CURVES, FROM THE STAIR-WELL OPENING DOWN TO THE FLOOR. THE SINUOUS CURVE OF A SLENDER RAILING ADDS TO THE SENSE OF WEIGHT-LESSNESS, WHILE THE BALUS-TERS ARE PLAIN SQUARE SPINDLES THAT DO NOT TO DRAW ATTENTION AWAY FROM THE ELEGANT CURVES. NOT ONLY DOES THE RAILING END IN A CHARACTERISTIC VOLUTE BUT ALSO THE START-ING STEP BENEATH IT ECHOES THE SHAPE.

STYLE NOTES

Polyurethane is the common choice for finishing wooden railings because it is durable and easy to apply. It is attractive in its own right, but it lacks some of the subtlety and softness of a traditional hand-rubbed finish. For a truly classic antique look on a fine hardwood railing, try rubbing in several coats of tung oil instead of polyurethane. It's less durable, but it looks amazing—and you probably won't mind the soothing task of rubbing oil into hardwood once a year anyway.

SOMETIMES A BIT OF THE
UNEXPECTED IS A WELCOME
TOUCH. A HEAVY ROPE
STRETCHED BETWEEN BOX
NEWELS SERVES A RAILING ON
THIS BASEMENT-TO-BED-
ROOMS STAIRCASE.

A FULLY ENCLOSED STAIRWAY IS BY NO MEANS A LOST CAUSE WHEN IT COMES TO STYLE. BY EXTENDING THE RUN A FEW STEPS BEYOND THE WALLS, THIS STAIRCASE GETS A DRAMATIC CASCADE OF STARTING STEPS. BRACKETED RAILINGS NEEDN'T BE BORING CONCESSIONS TO BUILDING CODE; THESE ARE MADE OF BEAUTIFUL HARDWOOD, WITH CLEVER GOOSENECK EXTENSIONS.

Through the Post

Another common way to secure a rail is to run the railing over the balusters but into or through massive newel posts—hence the descriptive name given them: *through the post*. This style is most common in stairs that make 90- or 180-degree turns, like switchbacks or *L*s. The massive forms of Arts and Crafts–style stairs or the intricate carving of Victorian stairs are particularly suited to this kind of railing, as it emphasizes the newel post and leaves the top free for a cap or finial (or a light, as you'll soon see). In this arrangement, hardwood profiled to a comfortable shape is an excellent choice, but because the railing is supported by large newels, more unconventional materials from simple copper tubing to rope to driftwood are all options for an eclectic look.

Wall Brackets

The final common way to secure a railing is the least celebrated and used. Where one or both sides of a stair are bounded by a wall, building codes often require a railing attached to the walls with brackets. More often than not, the railing and brackets are cheap in construction and uninteresting to look at-little more than a wooden dowel on a brass bracket (homeowners have been known to take these down as soon as the building inspector is out the door). However, with a little creativity, it is possible to design and build a wall railing worthy of notice. For enclosed stairs, consider trcating the railing like an over-the-post design by extending it beyond the entrance to the stairwell and finishing it with a traditional volute.

ACCESSIBLE RAILINGS

Railings aren't a mere aesthetic detail. A poorly positioned railing—or an absent railing—can make a staircase inaccessible to people who are elderly or disabled, and dangerous for children. A loose railing can be downright hazardous. Railings should be easy to grip—1½ inches (4 cm) around

and 1½ inches (4 cm) from the wall is good-and between 30 and 36 inches (0.75–1 m) from the treads. If a member of the household is quite short, it may be useful to install a lower railing as well. If a partially enclosed stair does not have a railing along its wall, consider adding one.

THIS STAIRCASE FEATURES A DISTINCTIVE NEGATIVE-SPACE RAILING TREATMENT. THE RAIL IS FORMED BY A CUTOUT IN THE PLYWOOD PANELS THAT FORM THE BALUSTRADE.

Balusters

Balusters are, at their simplest, slender posts that connect the railing to the treads. Individually, they're not much to contemplate, but the average staircase has a couple dozen of them, usually two or three per tread, or however many are necessary to keep the spacing at less than 4 inches (10 cm), as mandated by most codes.

When most people hear the word *baluster*, a lathe-turned spindle of wood instantly springs to mind—and not without good reason; attractive turned spindles are common in most styles and are widely available. Variations on this theme include balustrades with several baluster profiles arranged in a pattern, such as closely spaced, thin wooden dowels and delicate spindles of wrought iron.

Historically, balusters have strayed far from the familiar spindle pattern. Some balustrades even discard individual balusters entirely in favor of continuous panels of everything from web-like wrought iron to carved wood to ceramic tile to tempered glass. A traditional Arts and Crafts–style version of panel balusters uses closely spaced wooden slats. Adjoining sides of individual slats are sometimes cut out with mirror-image halves of a pattern or shaped to render the decoration. Once you start thinking in these terms, a nearly endless variety of effects becomes available.

THE BALUSTERS AND NEWEL ON THIS STAIRCASE ARE ARCHETYPAL CRAFTSMAN STYLE. THE PATTERN OF THE CLOSELY SPACED HORIZONTAL AND VERTICAL SLATS ECHO THE LEADING ON THE LEADED-GLASS WINDOWS.

SOMEHOW, NEOCLASSICAL
TURNINGS JUST WOULDN'T
DO FOR BALUSTERS ON A LOG
STAIRCASE IN A LOG CABIN,
SO A CRAFTY CARPENTER
WENT "WHOLE LOG" AND
CAREFULLY SELECTED AND
FINISHED BRANCHES TO DO
THE JOB.

THE MASSIVE STAIRCASE IN
THIS PRAIRIE-STYLE HOME IS
FILLED WITH LITTLE DETAILS
THAT BREAK WITH CONVEN-
TION—ALL TO GOOD EFFECT.
INSTEAD OF A NEWEL, THE
STAIR-STEP RAILING TERMI-
NATES AT A FULL-HEIGHT POST.

Landings

With careful planning and clever design, a landing can be a staircase's most useful and attractive detail. With a little work, almost any landing can be a space for decoration, storage, or a small sitting or reading nook.

At a minimum, a landing should provide a comfortable place to pause. A window provides a view and helps make this possible. But touches as simple as a few paintings or photographs or a mirror also encourage travelers to pause. Bookshelves, either built-in or freestanding, or a window seat are other good ways to make use of a landing; these elements offer both storage and design advantages.

Landing Living Spaces

It takes surprisingly little square footage for a landing to go from a short pause on the way up to a destination all its own. Federal- and Georgian-style houses often had very large landings complete with windows and chairs. With any staircase that has a large landing—or if you're designing a new staircase—think of the landing as a small room. Adding a window will go a long way toward establishing the space. If a landing already has a window, consider adding a pane of stained or etched glass to create a focal point.

To transform a landing into a small room, you can design the staircase such that the landing can continue beyond the minimum space required. This can be accomplished by means of a large bay window or even a full-fledged bump-out in the exterior wall. It may also be possible to expand the landing into an adjoining space. Perhaps the most extravagant way to enhance a landing is by adding a walkout balcony.

Something as simple as adding a bench under the window and a few family photographs might turn the landing into a warm and sunny seating area, fit for full-fledged napping rather than just a moment's pause.

Under the Stairs

Recapturing the space under a staircase has been a goal of architects and remodelers probably forever, and they have invented a great variety of creative solutions: bookshelves, closets, bathrooms—even living quarters for young wizards like the children's book character Harry Potter, who famously lived in a cupboard under the stairs for his first ten years.

Depending on how a set of stairs is laid out, a great deal of useable space may be gained by keeping some of the stair framing open. Straight stairs in large, old homes have the most potential for usable space—there's often room for a half-bath—but other layouts can also accommodate built-in shelving or seating, or even a gas fireplace.

BUNGALOWS TEND TO ENCOURAGE A SORT OF SPATIAL ECONOMY LUST; THEIR OWNERS ARE LIKELY TO LOOK AT A WALL AND WONDER WHY IT DOESN'T HAVE A BUILT-IN BOOKCASE. THE STAIRCASE ABOVE IS A GOOD EXAMPLE. AN EXCELLENT CHEST OF DRAWERS IS BUILT INTO OTHERWISE DEAD SPACE UNDER THE LANDING.

THE INGENIOUS VENTILATION SYSTEMS OF MODERN GAS FIREPLACES, AS SHOWN ABOVE, ALLOW FOR CREATIVE PLACEMENT OF GAS STOVES AND FIREPLACES—INCLUDING, OF COURSE, UNDER STAIRCASES. HERE, THE REST OF THE SPACE IS DEVOTED TO BUILT-IN BOOKSHELVES.

SIX

OUTDOOR STAIRS

BIG STAIRS GO WELL WITH A BIG FAÇADE. THE FRONT OF THIS HOUSE HAS DISTINCT ECHOES OF AN ANCIENT GREEK TEMPLE, AND THE FULL-WIDTH FRONT STAIRS ARE AN APPROPRIATE TOUCH. THE LOWER, UNCOVERED LEVEL OF THE PORCH INTER-RUPTS THE STAIRS IN THE MIDDLE AND ADDS A SUNNY SEATING SPACE.

Well before humans built houses with two stories (much less conceived staircases to go between them), people stacked wood, stone, or earth itself to make climbing and descending hills, cliffs, and even mountains, if not easy, at least bearable. Outdoor stairs are truly the original stairways. Most houses have at least one set of stairs outdoors, and many have three or four. They're all well worth a bit of stairscaping.

STEEL SPIRAL STAIRCASES ARE AVAILABLE WITH FINISHES DURABLE ENOUGH FOR OUTDOOR USE. A SPIRAL STAIR IS A GREAT WAY TO PROVIDE ACCESS TO A GARDEN OR PATIO FROM A RAISED DECK— OR EVEN FROM A BEDROOM BALCONY;

STYLE NOTES

Whatever the style, it's a good idea to be generous with the top landing on a front stair, especially if it will be fitted with a storm door. It needs to be deep and wide. Nothing is more frustrating than having to walk backward down the stairs, fumbling with two bags of groceries, because the door swings toward you and the landing isn't wide or deep enough to accommodate it.

Front Door Stairs

Transitional spaces—entryways and halls—are crucial spaces in architecture. Interior staircases are a case in point, and so are stairs that lead to front doors. Think of the classic big-city brownstone or apartment building. People inevitably gather on the steps on pleasant summer evenings.

Stairs make a front door a destination, almost a stage, serving the same purpose as a landing on a well-designed interior stair. The front porch landing is the place where guests meet you and your home. One way to design such a stair, found on many traditionally styled homes, is with a combination of a walkway and stairs (more walkway if the front yard is fairly level; more stairs if it is sloped) leading more or less directly to the front door. In most neoclassical

designs, the landing at the top of the stair is covered, generally with a portico that features architectural details that complement the rest of the house. Symmetry is maintained, often to such a degree that on opening the front door, what a visitor sees first is the formal interior staircase.

Exterior stairs of this sort can be made of wood, stone, or concrete. Details such as railings and balusters can be fabricated from wood or iron to match the exterior architectural details.

In a home with a plain façade, the front stairs present an opportunity to add architectural interest. Columned porticos and curved starting steps are just two ways to add a touch of design.

CUT STONE STAIRS WIND
THROUGH THE LANDSCAPING
TOWARD THE FRONT DOOR
OF THIS HOUSE, COMFORT-
ABLY TUCKED UNDER THE
EAVES OF A LOW-SLUNG
ROOF. THIS MEANDERING
APPROACH IS PERFECTLY
SYMPATHETIC WITH THE
COZY, PRIVATE FAÇADE.

Private and Informal Entrances

Another school of thought takes a slightly different approach to the front door—literally and figuratively. Houses need not always present themselves as open to the world. The houses of the turn-of-the-twentieth-century Prairie School, most famously those designed by Frank Lloyd Wright, are good examples. They are approached via circuitous and often partially enclosed walkways to front doors that often seem deliberately hidden. Wright described this sort of meandering walkway to the front door as a "pathway to discovery." It's also true that by prolonging the approach to the house, the visitor can spend more time appreciating its exterior.

This entryway style created a sense of privacy that Wright thought was suitable for houses in urban settings. To Wright's mind, a house is not a public building, and the public doesn't need an invitation from the street. There are other advantages to a less direct and more mysterious path to the front door. It allows the walkway to integrate naturally with the landscape and, as with a curved, sweeping staircase, allows for a more dramatic, deliberate approach. When done well, the effect isn't one of delay but rather of a gradual transition from indoors to out.

Where the site of a house permits, several short flights of stairs are an excellent

way to get this effect, prolonging the approach to create a Wrightian "pathway of discovery." Instead of mounting to the door in a single, straight flight, the stairs can be distributed over several small sections that approach the door somewhat indirectly. This allows the front walkway to integrate naturally with landscaping features that favor curved paths over straight. Consider stone, brick, or concrete to create a combination of short flights and long landings.

SIMPLE, OPEN-RISER, DECK-STYLE STAIRS LEAD THE WAY UP A HILLSIDE TO THIS SECLUDED CABIN. AMPLE LANDINGS AND STURDY HANDRAILS ARE CRITICAL FOR LONG STAIRWAYS. NOTICE THE STEEL CABLES USED INSTEAD OF WOOD SLATS, OR BALUSTERS, BELOW THE RAILING. THEY PROVIDE JUST AS MUCH STABILITY BUT ARE MUCH LESS CONSPICUOUS—A GOOD THING WHEN YOU WANT A STAIRCASE TO BLEND IN WITH THE LANDSCAPE.

Ergonomics and Safety

Whatever the style, ergonomics and safety are crucial elements of a front door stairway. When done correctly, stairs make it easy to greet visitors comfortably and to get through the door with grocery bags in both hands in a rainstorm. When poorly designed, front steps can be downright hazardous.

As with all stairs, landings should be securely attached and easy for all to use. Treads should conform to the same standards as interior stairs, and, where climate necessitates, should be treated to prevent slips and falls in icy weather.

The landing must be large enough for at least two people to stand on comfortably. When the front door has a storm door, this is doubly important. If the landing isn't deep enough, people will have to step backward down the stairs when the door swings open (this is, as noted, particularly unpleasant when one's arms are full of grocery bags). Covering the landing before the front door with a roof or awning not only provides shelter for visitors but also it makes the house seem to extend a welcome to guests.

LOGS MAKE A BOLD STATEMENT AS EXTERIOR STAIRS, ESPECIALLY AGAINST THIS STONE RETAINING WALL. THE RAIL IS A PARTICULARLY IMPRESSIVE DETAIL, AS IT IS MADE FROM A SINGLE BRANCH STRIPPED OF BARK TO PROVIDE A COMFORTABLE HANDHOLD.

COLORFUL CERAMIC TILES AND WARM, NONSLIP TERRA-COTTA PAVERS COMBINE TO FINISH A CONCRETE FRONT STAIR ON THIS GRACIOUS MEDITERRANEAN ENTRYWAY. THE GENTLE CURVE OF THE STAIR MAKES THE APPROACH A LITTLE MORE MYSTERIOUS AND INTERESTING THAN A STRAIGHT FLIGHT, AND IT COMPLEMENTS THE ARCHES OF THE FRONT DOOR.

A Little Excitement for Concrete Stairs

Poured or precast concrete stairs lead the way up to millions of front doors. Concrete steps have a number of advantages: they're low-maintenance and, when properly constructed and installed, long-wearing. They also integrate well with concrete walkways and sidewalks. Unfortunately, they're often dull gray masses on the fronts of otherwise stylish homes. Cast-iron railings can add a decorative touch, but the sheer mass of concrete inevitably draws attention to itself.

Fortunately, there are a number of ways to dress up concrete while retaining the material's practical advantages.

Concrete is a good base for ceramic tile. As a long as the concrete surface is smooth and free of cracks, adding tile to the risers and even the treads is probably easier than tiling a bathroom. Consult a tile retailer about tiles suitable for traffic and exposure to the elements. Consider an

unglazed tile with a good deal of texture for treads and use highly glazed, decorative painted tiles for risers.

Garden Stairs

Large garden stairs that descend a long distance can be formed from concrete or treated lumber, or they may be framed like decks. For more gradual slopes or stairs that need to blend readily into the landscape, stone or brick pavers are ideal.

Straight runs of stairs, and those with landings and switchbacks at right angles, are appropriate for the geometric layouts of formal gardens and when used near tra-ditionally styled houses. Curving or winding stairs, which are more informal in appearance, are well suited to landscapes that are natural looking and those influenced by Asian design principles. Curving stairs complement contemporary houses or those with asymmetric designs.

THE GLASS TILES EMBEDDED IN THIS LANDING ALLOW LIGHT TO FILTER TO THE POTTING SHED BUILT UNDER-NEATH THE STAIRCASE— AN ELEMENT OF FUNCTIONAL DESIGN THAT SERVES A DUAL PURPOSE. TRULY GREAT GARDEN STAIRS DISAPPEAR INTO THE LANDSCAPE WHILE ENHANCING THE OVERALL EFFECT.

GARDEN STAIRS WORK BEST
WHEN THEY INTEGRATE WITH
THEIR SURROUNDINGS. STONE
BLOCKS DEFINE EARTH STAIRS
AS THEY WIND THROUGH THIS
WOODED LANDSCAPE. SIMPLE
LIGHTS OUTLINE THE STAIRS
AND ACCENT THE PLANTS.

THE STONE STAIRS OF MOUNT SINAI

According to the Bible, Moses received the Ten Commandments on the top of Mount Sinai, in what is now Egypt. Centuries later, people began making pilgrimages to the summit of Mount Sinai. To ease the climb to the summit, the monks who inhabited the monastery of Saint Catherine at the foot of the mountain built a stone stairway that winds its way to the summit, using nearly 4,000 steps to ascend over 7,000 feet (2,134 m). Over a millennium later, pilgrims, tourists, and the occasional camel still climb these rough stairs, often beginning just after midnight in order to arrive at the summit in time to see the sun rise over the Gulf of Aqaba. (A few still honor the ascetic tradition of climbing the last 1,000 stairs on their knees.) It's undoubtedly one of the most amazing stairways in the world.

STONE IS THE MOST ANCIENT OF ALL STAIR MATERIALS AND IS STILL AMONG THE MOST ATTRACTIVE. THESE SIMPLE STONE STEPS FOLLOW THE PATH OF THE STAIR-STEP WATERFALL WITHOUT ADDING A LOT OF DISTRACTING MATERIAL TO THE LANDSCAPE.

Deck Stairs

Decks have come a long way from their humble origins as simple wooden platforms with room for a charcoal grill and maybe a picnic table. Modern decks can be sprawling structures encompassing several levels and including kitchens, hot tubs, dining spaces, common spaces, and more. Decks are, more than ever, outdoor living spaces for large numbers of families.

Although walls obviously are not desirable for dividing exterior rooms on large decks, undefined spaces tend to make people uncomfortable. Stairs can do the important job of helping define deck spaces. Short flights of stairs direct traffic from the dining space to the hot

tub, providing the visual and physical separation necessary for people to feel at ease in each. Cascading stairs ease the transition between the deck and the ground below and are visually more appealing than an open space below the deck.

Decks are often made of a single material, so from a distance, a large, flat deck can look uninteresting and unbalanced compared to the rest of the house. Multiple levels, and thus stairs and railings, give decks shape, dimension, and greater visual appeal. As you would when designing an indoor stair, consider main deck stairs a separate, important space. Consider the details. When made of

different materials than those of the main decking, treads, railings, and balusters can lend a good deal of attractive detail to a deck.

Like stairs, modern decks need not be limited to traditional wood for all components. Metals and composite materials are increasingly prevalent, and they add an additional flexibility to stair and deck design.

SPIRAL STAIRS CAN MAKE
ABOVEGROUND EXTERIOR
SPACES LIKE THESE MORE
ACCESSIBLE AND USEFUL.
HERE, THE BOLD RED STAIRS
SEEM TO SPROUT FROM
THE GARDEN, A STRIKING
SPLASH OF COLOR AGAINST
THE WHITE EXTERIOR OF
THE HOUSE.

Two-Story Decks

Outdoor spaces that mirror indoor ones are increasingly common in modern houses, so it's no surprise that cantilevered decks and patios are sprouting from the second floors of many homes. Adding an exterior spiral stair to a space otherwise accessible only from indoors adds a new dimension of usability without the intrusively large structure of a regular stair. Imagine being able to grill on a first-floor patio and serve the food on a table on a second-story deck—without carrying it through the house. For an outdoor lifestyle, it makes a good deal of sense to be able to access all outdoor living spaces without having to traipse through the house.

Spiral stairs can sit beside the second-story platform, or they can rise from directly beneath and enter within the platform. Low-maintenance prefabricated metal spiral stairs suitable for exterior installation are available in many styles and colors (see Resources on page 174).

SEVEN

REPAIRING AND RESTORING STAIRCASES

In a great many old houses the original stairway is buried under decades of wear and more than a few ill-advised paint jobs and remodeling projects. Because the staircase is often the centerpiece of a house and the professional calling card of its builder, restoring such a staircase to its former glory may be well worth the time and effort required.

This chapter will help you assess the condition of your stairs and decide just what kind of work they will require. Along the way, you'll find advice on fixing and repairing stairs as well as how to proceed with instructions about a full-scale makeover.

IT'S A MODEST FARMHOUSE BACK STAIR, THE KIND THAT MIGHT BE BURIED UNDER CARPET OR A COAT OR TWO OF HARVEST GOLD PAINT. THIS ONE, THOUGH, HAS BEEN THOUGHTFULLY CARED FOR. THE WORN OLD TREADS ARE FINISHED JUST ENOUGH TO SHOW THEIR YEARS BEAUTIFULLY, AND SIMPLE BEADBOARD MAKES AN IDEAL WALL COVERING. THE BIRCH BRANCH RAILING GIVES A TOUCH OF PERSONALITY.

IF YOU SEE A GAP IN THE
JOINT BETWEEN A TREAD AND
THE RISER BELOW IT, CARE-
FULLY DRIVE HARDWOOD
SHIMS COATED WITH GLUE
INTO THE SPACE. USE A UTIL-
ITY KNIFE TO CUT OFF EXCESS
SHIM MATERIAL.

REPAIRING SQUEAKS

Squeaky stairs have a certain cinematic appeal—they're excellent for alerting you to the presence of an intruder at the last possible second. In everyday life, however, persistent squeaks and creaks can quickly lose their charm. Further, a creaky, badly worn staircase is likely not a safe staircase. Damaged treads and loose balusters can cause falls and should be addressed to prevent accidents.

Fortunately, squeaks are easy to fix, especially if you have access to the underside of the stairs as is sometimes the case when the main stair sits directly above an unfinished basement stair. In such cases, squeaking treads can be fixed easily and invisibly. First, try to identify where the stair squeaks. Does it squeak when weight is on the front of the tread? Or the back?

Front-of-Stair Squeaks

If the front of the tread squeaks, there's probably some play in the joint between the tread and the riser below it; a gap may even be visible from the underside. If you can see the gap, drive wooden shims coated with wood glue into the space so they are snug but do not enlarge the gap or push through the front of the stair. Use a utility knife to cut off the exposed end of the shim. It's also a good idea to cut short pieces of 1 x 1 lumber and secure them as a brace in the joint between the tread and riser. Cut the brace to the width of the tread and coat two adjacent sides with construction adhesive or wood glue. Press the brace against the tread-riser joint. Finally, drill pilot holes through the brace and drive wood screws through them to attach the brace to the back of the riser and to the underside of the tread. Be sure to use screws short enough not to come through the top side of the stair.

INSTALLING QUARTER-ROUND MOLDING CAN SILENCE A SQUEAKY JOINT BETWEEN A TREAD AND A RISER. IT ALSO LOOKS GREAT (WHICH IS GOOD, BECAUSE YOU'LL NEED TO DO IT ON EVERY STEP). COAT THE FLAT SIDES WITH CONSTRUCTION ADHESIVE, POSITION THE MOLDING, AND DRIVE FINISH NAILS AT A SLIGHT ANGLE THROUGH THE MOLDING AND INTO THE TREAD AND RISER.

Back-of-Stair Squeaks

If the back of the tread squeaks, it's likely that the joint between the tread and the riser above it is not as secure as it once was. Fix this by carefully drilling pilot holes for 2-inch (5 cm) deck screws at regular intervals through the back side of the riser into the back edge of the tread; drill slowly to avoid splitting the tread. Drive screws carefully into the pilot holes to secure the tread and riser.

Special Considerations

If you do not have access to the underside of a staircase, effective repairs are still possible, but some care is required to conceal them. The basic technique is simple: drill pilot holes for screws through the front of the tread and into the top edge of the riser. Drill the holes at a slight angle to give the screws more holding power. If the staircase has a runner that can be removed, drive the screws under the runner. If the

treads are completely exposed, counterbore the pilot hole so the screw head sits a little below the surface of the tread, and then cover the screw head with colored wood filler to match the tread. You can make the repair even less conspicuous by using a screw with a snap-off head (Squeeeeek No More is a common brand). These fasteners have the holding power of screws, but after they are driven, the screw head snaps off, leaving a hole the size of a finish nail—which is much easier to conceal (but nearly impossible to remove, so take care when driving). These screws are ideal for repairing squeaks on carpeted stairs.

It's also possible to firm up the joint at the back of a tread from above (and often dress up the stairs in the process). Cut pieces of matching quarter-round molding as wide as the treads. Paint or stain as desired. Coat the flat sides with adhesive and place the molding in the joint between the tread and the riser above it. Drill pilot

holes for finish nails. Drill pairs of holes so that one nail goes at a slight angle into the tread and the other goes at a slight angle into the riser. Drive the nails and countersink them with a nail set. (If you have a nail gun, you can skip the pilot holes and countersinking.) Fill the holes with colored wood filler. Bear in mind that if you do this repair for one squeaky stair, you'll likely want to do it for all the others, even if they don't squeak, to keep the look consistent.

WITH THE FILLET REMOVED, DRIVE A SHORT DECK SCREW THROUGH THE TOP OF THE BALUSTER AND INTO THE RAILING. A CLAMP HELPS KEEP THE BALUSTER FROM MOVING WHILE YOU DRILL.

Repairing Balustrades

Another common staircase malady is loose or damaged baluster components. A loose newel cap (or one that comes off entirely) or a rattling baluster might begin to grow on you after a while, but it's better to keep a balustrade in good condition because a loose one presents a potential hazard. Fortunately, it's fairly simple to repair, replace, and restore individual parts of a balustrade without redoing the whole thing.

Most balusters have square ends and are attached to the underside of the railing with glue and finish nails. A piece of trim called a fillet often fills the space between each baluster and provides additional stability (less often, a continuous piece of trim runs on either side of the bottom of the rail, and the square ends of the balusters fit in between). The bottom end of most balusters connects directly to the tread below by means of a round peg that fits into a hole bored in the tread—often in the joint between the tread and the piece of trim that caps the tread's edge.

Over time, any of these connections can loosen, allowing balusters to rattle or even twist and break.

Fixing Loose Balusters

If a baluster is loose but otherwise undamaged, fixing it simply requires reinforcing the connection. Carefully remove the fillet above the loose baluster (a hammer, a chisel, and patience are the best tools, and you'll probably need to replace the fillet). Secure the baluster by driving a short deck screw at an angle through the top of the baluster (the part that will be concealed by the new fillet) and into the railing. It's a good idea to secure the other side of the baluster with a block of wood or a clamp. Secure the new fillet with wood glue and finish nails.

A loose baluster can quickly become a broken baluster, especially if the staircase doubles as a jungle gym for children. Luckily, most home centers and woodworking stores carry a wide selection of common baluster types and can typically order less common ones or at least recommend a cabinetmaker who can make copies. Carefully remove the broken baluster (you may want to cut it in half to make removal easier) and wiggle it loose from the tread and railing (you may need to remove existing nails or pegs). Scrape out any glue or wood chips that adhere the railing and tread.

ARCHITECTURAL SALVAGE

For the adventurous soul in search of something really unusual, architectural salvage dealers and online auctions offer another option for replacement balusters. At salvage yards, it's not at all uncommon to find bins full of staircase and porch balusters saved from demolished old buildings. If you have basic carpentry skills and some experience with finishes, adapting salvaged balusters to an existing balustrade is not difficult. And remember, not all balusters need to match. Neoclassical and Victorian staircases frequently featured two or more baluster profiles arranged in a repeating pattern.

GLUE BOTH ENDS OF THE NEW BALUSTER. SET THE BOTTOM DOWEL IN THE TREAD FIRST, AND THEN FIT THE TOP DOWEL INTO THE RAILING.

Replacing Broken Balusters

Most replacement balusters come with extra-long square sections at the top and bottom to accommodate a variety of railing heights. Cut the top and bottom ends to fit your balustrade. The top end will probably be cut at an angle. Use a *T*-bevel or the old baluster to determine the correct angle.

To install the replacement baluster, apply glue to both ends and fit the dowel on the bottom into the socket in the tread (you may need to remove a piece of trim on the end of the tread). Set the top of the baluster in its slot and secure it with a deck screw as described above. Replace the fillets as described previously and finish the new baluster to match.

Fixing Loose Railings

It's also possible for the connection between the railing and the newel or the railing and the wall to come loose.

This is particularly dangerous because it compromises the entire balustrade.

Railings connect to newels in a variety of ways, some of which may require the services of an experienced carpenter to fix. One common and fairly easily accessible connection method uses a bolt embedded in the side of the newel and the end of the rail. A nut in the railing keeps the bolt tight and secures the railing to the newel. If this is the case, look for a concealed access plug on the underside of the railing. Drill a hole in the plug and remove it with a chisel to gain access to the nut. Tighten the nut until the railing is secure. You can make a replacement plug by cutting a section from a dowel of the same diameter, or you can purchase one at a woodworking store.

The Staircase Makeover

In the influential book *A Pattern Language*, architect and author Christopher Alexander suggests that a well-designed staircase should serve as a stage—a dynamic focal point for the house. It's hard for a tired and uninspired staircase to fill this role, and if it seems as if your staircase falls short of its dramatic potential but is otherwise adequate for the space, a cosmetic makeover might be the answer.

The parts of a staircase that you can see are less important, technically, than the framing that lies beneath. If the framing—the staircase's bones, so to speak—is sound and the layout suits the house's needs, a drab staircase is an excellent candidate for a makeover.

Home centers carry an astonishing variety of treads, trim, railings, balusters, and newels. If this book has whetted your appetite for something farther off the beaten track, a local cabinetmaker or staircase carpenter can help bring your ideas to fruition.

Refinishing

Many houses already have beautiful staircases; they're just hidden. A makeover might be as simple as stripping old paint and refinishing. In older homes, nice woodwork was the rule, not the exception, so layers of paint, varnish, and grime often conceal beautiful red oak treads or dark mahogany railings.

It's not always easy to tell whether the wood beneath an old paint job is worth exposing. Lift carpeting or trim to find spots of unfinished wood. Use sandpaper or a small amount of paint stripper to remove the finish in an inconspicuous place for a clue as to what's under the paint. You may be pleasantly surprised.

Keep in mind, though, that in older houses it isn't at all unusual to find beautiful oak treads, newel caps, and railings paired with less distinctive pine or ash risers, balusters, and newels. Builders often economized by saving the fine stained hardwoods for the focal points and using painted lesser woods for everything else. If you lift 30-year-old carpeting and strike gold with pristine oak treads, don't automatically assume that the rest of the staircase is made of the same material. Check a small patch before slathering on the stripper or plugging in the heat gun.

Safety Precautions

Stripping paint from a staircase, especially in an older house, requires care and planning. First, if a surface was painted before 1980, it is likely that the paint contains lead, a very hazardous substance. It is important not to create excess dust when removing this paint and disposing of the waste. You can hire refinishing professionals to strip woodwork or you can do the work yourself, as long as you have proper protective gear, good ventilation, and dust control. Check with your local building department for guidelines on working with and disposing of lead paint.

Stripping some parts of a staircase might be so labor-intensive that it makes more sense to replace them. Intricate turned balusters are notoriously difficult to strip. Before you go to the effort of hand-stripping dozens of balusters, check your local home center or woodworking store. Identical unfinished balusters may be available for less than the cost of the time and effort required to strip old ones. If the balusters are unique and you can remove them from the balustrade, a furniture-stripping specialist can remove the paint for a fee.

A SIMPLE *L*-SHAPED STAIRCASE
CAN BE STRIKINGLY MADE
OVER FROM LUMBER AND
PARTS AVAILABLE AT HOME
CENTERS. REMOVE OLD
TREADS AND RISERS AND
REPLACE THEM WITH LONG-
WEARING, PRECUT SOLID OAK
REPLACEMENTS (*A*). DRESS UP
THE PLAIN OPEN WALL OF
THE SECOND FLIGHT WITH
NARROW MOLDING FOR A PIC-
TURE-FRAME EFFECT (*B*).
REPLACE STRAIGHT BALUS-
TERS WITH A GRID OF NAR-
ROW HARDWOOD PANELS (*C*).
CAP THE BALUSTERS WITH A
STAINED SOLID OAK RAILING
(*D*). INSTEAD OF A RAILING AT
THE SIDE OF THE LANDING,
BUILD A FULL-HEIGHT SCREEN
THAT ECHOES THE GRIDWORK
BALUSTRADE (*E*).

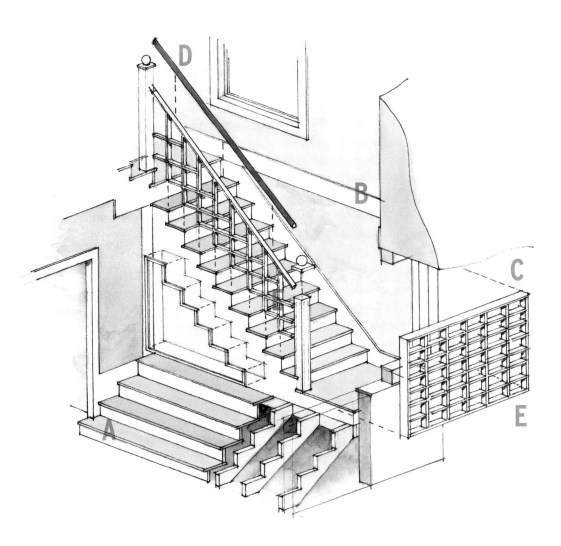

Retrimming

Staircases don't exactly come apart like
Legos, but parts are surprisingly inter-
changeable. An anonymous carpeted staircase with a bland railing can be
transformed into a fancy Colonial-style
staircase complete with hardwood treads
and turned balusters by means of precut
materials available at home centers for a
small fraction of the cost of a complete
replacement.

The treads, balusters, railings, and
trim on most staircases can be removed
with simple hand tools (and a little
patience). Replace them with precut and
unfinished staircase parts from a home
center or woodworking store or hire trim
carpenters to install custom finishing

pieces. Newel posts can also be replaced;
those that are attached to the floor joists
with bolts, however, are difficult to remove.

Remodeling a staircase is an excellent
excuse to improve lighting; it's easy to add
lighting when walls and framing are open.
Many older staircases are insufficiently or
unattractively lit, and the existing lights
may lack adequate controls. Adding a few
wall sconces or an eye-catching hanging
fixture can make an enormous difference.
After all, you'll want to be able to see the
finished creation.

STYLE NOTES

If you plan to paint your newly
installed trimwork, consider using
moldings made from urethane instead
of real wood. Urethane doesn't
expand or contract over time, is easy
to cut, and is forgiving during installation. Many sorts of staircase trim
pieces are available in urethane at
home centers and through catalogs.

Walls Come Down

Several staircase layouts common in older houses have at least part of the stairs enclosed by a partition wall that separates them from the rest of the living space. This wall might be original to the house, or it might be the result of a remodel. Either way, such a wall can turn a perfectly good stairway into a boring hallway at best and a dark and gloomy one at worst.

Under most circumstances, such a wall can be opened up or even removed almost entirely. This has the effect not only of opening up the space but also making the staircase more of a focal point for the house.

A contractor can determine whether the wall is simply a partition (and thus easily altered) or whether it contains utilities or is structurally significant (and thus more expensive to alter).

THERE ARE SUBTLE DEGREES OF OPENNESS. REMOVING A STAIRCASE WALL ENTIRELY MAY BE NEITHER NECESSARY NOR DESIRABLE. THIS STAIR USES NARROW VERTICAL SLATS TO CREATE A SCREEN EFFECT, ADMITTING LIGHT WITHOUT MAKING THE STAIR-WELL ENTIRELY VISIBLE.

METAL BALUSTRADES

Wrought iron, steel, and aluminum
are viable alternatives to wooden
balusters when remodeling staircases.
Fabricators sell everything from individual balusters to panels to complete balustrades. Iron is an
authentic staircase material for several historical styles and can be
shaped in ways that complement
modern designs as well. Cast metal
also has the advantage of being both
strong and low-maintenance, as well
as very attractive. Further, it can
accept a variety of finishes.

WROUGHT-IRON PANELS LIKE
THESE ARE A QUICK AND COM-
PARATIVELY INEXPENSIVE WAY
TO ADD A DECORATIVE
TOUCH TO A STAIRCASE.
FACTORIES PRODUCE PANELS
AND BALUSTERS IN HUNDREDS
OF TRADITIONAL PATTERNS,
AND ARTISAN METALSMITHS
CAN FABRICATE BREATHTAK-
ING CREATIONS WORTHY OF
ANY STAIRCASE.

DO IT YOURSELF

In the pages that follow, you'll find step-by-step instructions to guide you through several common staircase upgrades. These projects require basic carpentry knowledge and familiarity with common hand tools but can all be completed in a weekend.

STYLE NOTES

One easy way to make a staircase more accessible for elderly family members or anyone with vision deficits is to paint the risers a color that contrasts with the treads. This makes the treads easy to see and helps prevent falls. Often it isn't a compromise at all, as it actually improves the appearance of the stair.

REMODELING FOR ACCESS

An excellent reason to remodel or modify an existing staircase is to improve its ergonomics and accessibility. A steep, narrow staircase, or one with an insufficient railing, can be a significant barrier for less mobile members of a household. If this is the case, consider hiring an architect or designer who specializes in accessible or universal design to help remodel your staircase. These professionals can help you identify improvements and alterations that can make getting up and down a staircase easier and safer for everyone. Options run the gamut from adding a second, lower railing to installing stair lifts or household elevators.

TOOLS AND SAFETY

These projects require basic carpentry and finishing tools. For installing trim, a compound miter saw and a power nailer will make the installation go much more smoothly and accurately. Both can be rented from tool rental centers listed in the business pages of your local telephone book.

Note: Always wear goggles whenever you work with tools, especially hammers or power nailers.

If your house was built before 1980, it probably contains lead paint. Dust and chips from lead paint are very hazardous, especially to children. Wear a respirator when sawing or sanding, and dispose of dust and paint chips in accordance with local rules regarding hazardous materials.

PROJECT:
Installing a Carpet Runner with Decorative Rods

MATERIALS LIST

Tape measure

Carpet padding

Carpet runner

Tackless strips

Decorative carpet runner rods

Carpet staples

Carpet knife

Latex glue

Knee kicker

Carpenter's square

Hacksaw (optional)

Adding a runner is a classic way to add color to a staircase. A carpet runner protects the high-traffic centers of hardwood treads while leaving the handsome varnished wooden ends of the treads exposed. A runner also provides a fair amount of noise reduction. Decorative rods don't actually do much to hold the runner down, but they look great.

Runners are generally installed with 3 inches (7.5 cm) of exposed tread on either side. For a tread 36 inches (1 m) wide, choose a 30-inch (0.75 m) runner. To determine the length of the runner, measure the height of one riser and the depth of one tread; add those numbers and multiply by the number of steps in the staircase; then add the height of one riser. Padding improves the feel of the runner and protects both carpet and treads from wear. Use a high-quality padding at least ¼ inch (6 mm) thick and order enough for each tread plus extra. Purchase enough tackless strips to cover the width of the runner multiplied by the number of treads, plus a little extra. Finally, specify decorative rods with a bracket width a bit wider than the runner.

Step 1

Install the tackless strips. Lightly mark the edge of the path of the runner on all the treads near the joint with the riser. Cut tackless strips 2 inches (5 cm) shorter than the width of the runner for each tread. For each tread, place a short piece of scrap tackless strip lengthwise at the back of tread so it is flush against the riser. Set a tackless strip against the spacer and nail it to the tread. Install tackless strips in this manner on each tread.

Step 2

To install the pad, cut pieces as wide as the runner and 2 inches (5 cm) longer than the tread depth. Staple one edge of the pad so it abuts the tackless strip. Pull the pad tight across the tread and secure it on the underside of the nosing with staples every 3 inches (7.5 cm)—ask the dealer about the appropriate size staple for your pad and carpet. Cut away any extra pad. Continue with the rest of the treads.

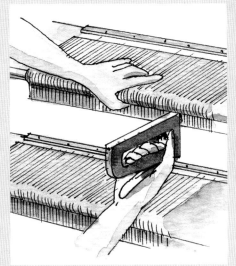

Step 3

Begin to attach the runner. Make sure the bottom edge of the runner is square. If it's not, use a carpet knife to trim it against a carpenter's square and secure any fraying fibers with latex glue. Lay the runner out on the first few stairs. Make sure it lines up with the reference marks. Butt the bottom edge of the runner up against the floor at the first riser. Secure the runner to the first riser by driving staples into the bottom of the riser every 3 inches (7.5 cm).

Step 4

Attach the runner to the first tread. Use a special tool called a knee kicker to stretch the carpet over the strips. Kickers can be rented where carpet is sold. Line up the runner between the reference marks and push it over the tackless strips. Place the kicker at the center of the runner a few inches back from the tread. Hold the knob on top of the kicker and hit the kicker forcefully with your knee. The carpet will tighten and catch on the strips. Move the kicker a couple of inches in either direction and repeat until the carpet is uniformly tight.

Step 5

Secure the carpet to the next riser. Use a carpet tool (a blunt-edged chisellike tool) to wedge the carpet firmly between the strips and the riser. Drive a staple into the edge of the runner just beyond the tackless strip on both sides. Also drive a staple through the edge of the runner a couple of inches above the tread. Repeat steps 4 and 5 for the rest of the stairs. At the last riser, trim the runner so it is square and flush with the underside of the tread or nose molding. Secure it with staples.

Step 6

Install the decorative rods. Attach the brackets at both edges of the runners near the tread-riser joint. Follow the manufacturer's directions for securing the brackets. If necessary, use a hacksaw to cut the rods to length. Secure them in the brackets. Install finials or caps on the brackets as instructed.

PROJECT:
Stenciling Risers

MATERIALS LIST

Mylar

Craft paper

Repositionable spray adhesive

Razor knife

Tape measure

Stencil brush

**Paints
(fast-drying acrylic craft
paints or latex interior paint)**

Painting or stenciling risers is a quick, inexpensive, and effective way to make over a set of stairs. Consider alternating a pattern and a solid color, or two different patterns, on every other riser for added interest.

Hundreds of ready-made stencils are available at craft and paint stores, or you can make your own. To make your own, print or copy your image or pattern onto paper. Secure the paper pattern to Mylar (a clear acetate sheet of stencil material) with spray adhesive. Cut out the pattern with a razor knife and then peel off and discard the paper.

You can test your pattern by printing it on a color printer and carefully cutting it out. Spray the back of the cutout pattern with repositionable spray adhesive and apply it to the stairs. Fine-tune the placement until you are satisfied, then take measurements for placing the actual stencil.

Step 1

Mark the center of each riser lightly at the top. Mark the center of the pattern on the stencil so you can line up the stencil on the mark on the risers. This ensures the stencil is centered every time. If you are using a multicolored pattern, mark each stencil so it will line up with the others on the center of the treads.

Step 2

Spray the back of the first stencil with a repositionable, water-soluble spray adhesive. Align the stencil carefully with the marks and press it firmly against the tread. Load a stencil brush lightly with paint and dab it over the stencil in a quick pouncing motion. It's a good idea to practice on a piece of scrap wood until you get the desired paint coverage and effect. After the stencil is covered, peel it away carefully from the tread before the paint is completely dry. Wipe away any excess paint and reapply the stencil in position on the next tread. Repeat for each tread. After the first stenciling is dry, apply any overlay stencils and paint in the same manner.

PROJECT:
Installing Picture-Frame Molding

MATERIALS LIST

Picture-frame molding

Compound miter saw or hacksaw and miter box

Paint or wood stain, sealer, and varnish

Wood glue

Finish nails

Power nailer or hammer and nail set

90-degree clamp

Wooden blocks

Putty

Caulk

Picture-frame molding is a classy addition to any room and a subtle and attractive way to dress up a staircase. See pages 20 and 69 for examples of picture-frame molding used to complement and enhance the lines of a set of stairs. On the open wall of a staircase, consider installing one frame that follows the contour of the steps. On a full wall, consider setting one edge of the frame back a few inches from the top edge of the skirtboard and creating a large triangular frame.

Picture-frame molding is available in solid wood and lightweight lookalike urethane at most home centers and lumberyards. Urethane molding is a fairly new product with many advantages: it's easy to cut, doesn't shrink or warp, and takes paint very well. It's an excellent choice, especially if you're inexperienced with installing trim. Many profiles are available in wood and urethane, but if you have picture-frame molding elsewhere on your walls, you may want to select a style that matches.

Step 1

Begin by marking the location of the frame on the walls. The way you lay out the frames depends largely on your staircase. The effect of the picture frame, however, comes off best when it is balanced on all sides, with the distance from all edges of the frame to a wall, floor, or stair tread being equal. Carefully measure the amount of picture frame molding needed and purchase 10 percent extra.

Step 2

Measure and cut the individual frame pieces. If you will be following the line of stairs on one side of the frame, as shown here and on page 20, cut all of the riser and tread pieces at the same time so that the length and miters are equal; these pieces will have a 45-degree miter on each end, facing opposite directions. A compound miter saw is useful for making precise, repetitive miter cuts, but you can also use a miter box and a hacksaw. Cut the long horizontal and vertical pieces to length, also with 45-degree miters, this time facing the same direction. If you're planning to paint or stain the pieces, do so now.

Step 3

Begin to assemble the frames. Small frames are much easier to assemble on the floor than on the wall. Assembling entire large frames may not be possible. In this case, assemble the frame in several manageable parts and assemble those parts of the frame on the wall. Join each miter with a dab of wood glue and a finish nail from each side. A power nailer is a great tool for this kind of delicate assembly. You can also use a hammer and a nail set. Hold the miters together with a 90-degree clamp and blocks when you drive the nails. Measure the finished corners to make sure they are square.

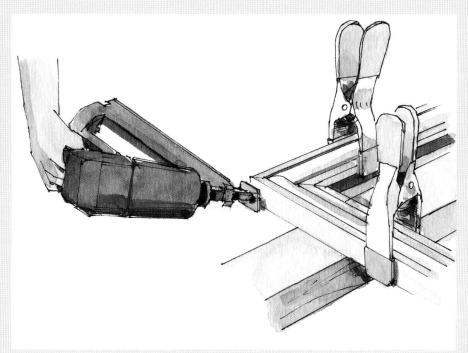

Step 4

Once the frames are assembled or partially assembled, dab the backs of each piece with construction adhesive. Press a frame onto the wall so it is aligned with the reference marks. Check the corners for square and level. Drive a few 1½-inch (4 cm) finish nails to secure the frame while the adhesive sets. Take care to wipe away any adhesive that squeezes out. Continue with the remaining piece or other frames, always checking for square and level as you go. Once all the frames are in place, set all the nails and cover them with putty. Caulk the joints between the frames and the wall. Touch up the paint as necessary.

PROJECT:
Installing a Shadow Rail

MATERIALS LIST

Chair rail molding

Cap molding

Paneling

Tape measure

Chalk line

Clamp

Circular saw

Two sawhorses

Stud finder

Finish nails

Power nailer or hammer and nail set

Construction glue

Primer

Paint

Putty

A shadow rail is essentially wainscoting along a wall that adjoins a flight of stairs. Rather than run horizontally, it runs diagonally, parallel with and at the same height as the stair rail—hence the term shadow rail. See pages 36 and 73 for examples. A shadow rail can be as simple as a crown molding installed to shadow the railing, or, for a more elaborate and substantial effect, tongue-and-groove paneling set beneath the chair rail. If the rest of the room has wainscoting of some kind, consider continuing the pattern on the stairs. You can also use a shadow rail to help blend in a real rail mounted on brackets.

Installing a shadow rail on a straight stair requires only basic carpentry skills. On stairs with landings, a shadow rail traditionally continues on the landing walls, running horizontally like normal wainscoting. This type of installation is a little more challenging, but the effect is worthwhile.

Chair rail molding is widely available in many profiles, both in wood and urethane (see page 76 for more on urethane molding). Beadboard is an excellent choice for informal or country-inspired paneling, as it's easy to cut and install.

To conceal the bottom edge of the paneling, you will probably need to install cap molding on top of the skirtboards. If necessary, remove the existing cap, and, after installing the paneling, replace the cap with a kind that covers the joint between the panel and the skirtboard.

Step 1

Mark the top of the shadow rail. Make marks on the wall at the top and bottom of each flight of stairs for the top of the paneling. Make the marks at the height of the actual railing minus the height of the chair rail you plan to use. (If you use chair rail designed to overlap the paneling—and most is—don't include the overlap in you measurement.) Snap a chalk line between all the marks. Measure from this line to the top of the baseboard (with the cap removed). Purchase enough paneling to cover this area, plus 25 percent. Purchase enough chair rail and baseboard cap to cover the length of the stairs, plus 10 percent.

Step 2

Cut the paneling to size. If you're using tongue-and-groove beadboard, keep in mind that you want the lines to run vertically, so make parallel angled cuts at the angle of the stairs (use a bevel gauge to measure it) at the top and bottom of each piece. You can cut several boards at once by laying them out together on sawhorse. Clamp a straight piece of scrap at the correct angle to the boards to act as a guide and cut the panels with a circular saw. Repeat for the top cut.

Step 3

Install the paneling. Begin at the bottom of the stairway. Mark a vertical line from the end of the shadow rail to the skirtboard below. Make a similar mark at the top of the stair. Cut two pieces of chair rail molding to the height of the top of the rail reference line. These are the vertical pieces that begin and end the shadow rail. You can also use pilasters and omit the miters on the top ends. Miter the bottoms of these piece with the stair angle (the same as the panels; see step 2). If you are using the chair rail molding for starting and ending pieces, miter the top ends of these pieces so they make a square corner with the diagonal chair rail molding (this miter is also determined by the angle of your stairs).

Make a wavy line of construction adhesive on the back of the starting piece. Place it against the vertical reference line and adjust it flush with the baseboard and lined up with the rail reference line. Check to make sure the piece is perfectly vertical. Secure it with a finish nail in the top and bottom. Install the first piece of paneling. Apply adhesive and fit it so its tongue edge is under the starting piece. Install the other pieces in the same manner, with tongues fitting snugly into grooves. Check for plumb as you go. Remember that the top and bottom of the panels will be covered, so the most important thing is that the lines be vertical. When you are less than the width of one piece from the vertical line at the top of the stairs, measure the width of the gap. Use a circular saw to rip, or vertically cut, a panel to the width of this space so the tongue edge of the paneling is wasted (remember to account for the depth of the groove). Place the final piece of paneling.

Step 4

Install the railing. Just above the rail reference line, use a stud finder to mark the stud locations. Cut the chair rail molding to length. You may need to use several pieces (molding comes in 8-foot lengths). To hide joints between pieces, cut the butting joints with mating 45-degree bevels, called scarf joints. Miter the top and bottom ends of the rail so they fit squarely with the starting and ending pieces. Set the first piece of rail on top of the paneling and against the matching miter on the start piece. Make sure it lines up with the reference marks and is parallel to the skirtboards. Secure the rail with a finish nail at each stud location. If the molding is hardwood, use a power nailer or drill pilot holes to prevent splitting. Install subsequent pieces in the same manner, making sure the last rail fits snugly with the ending piece. If necessary, cut new baseboard cap to fit and install it on the baseboard with finish nails. Set all nails with a nail set. Fill the nail holes with putty, and prime and paint the railing.

PART II

What Makes a Great Staircase?

EIGHT

GREAT STAIRS IN DETAIL

Sometimes you see a truly wonderful staircase in a magazine, or even in person, and you know it's impressive, but you just can't figure out what makes it extraordinary. Often, the answer is a confluence of dozens of small factors and seemingly minor details that make a large, complicated structure like a staircase—or a symphony—truly great.

In the pages that follow you'll find detailed drawings of some of the most beautiful and best-designed staircases in this book. Words and pictures call attention to the details and designs—from trim to siting to layout—that make them remarkable. As you brainstorm your own designs and begin to make rough sketches, you can flip through these pages for inspiration and insight into aspects of these staircases that you might wish to incorporate with your own project.

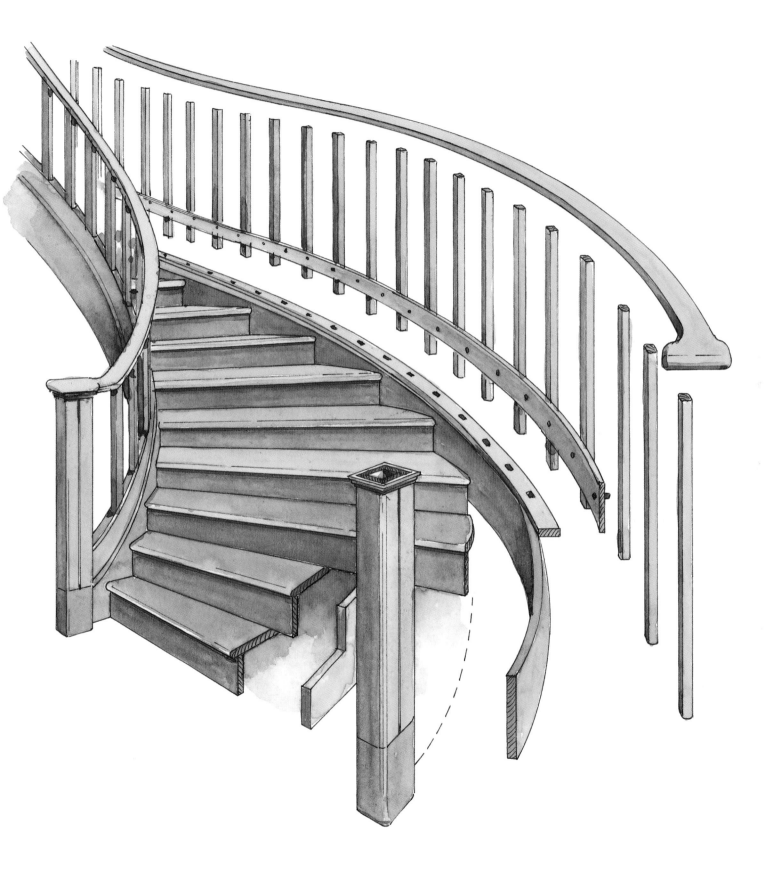

A Bit of an Enigma

There's a little bit of every design influence reflected in this enigma of a staircase. Leading almost straight to the hearth of a large brick fireplace, it has both a touch of Craftsman style and a touch of handyman. The room is a walk-out bedroom, but the staircase is a close relative of the garden-variety basement staircase. The woodwork is gorgeous, however, making it a perfect complement to the brick fireplace. *(Photograph, page 77)*

A

THE BUILT-INS

Building a dresser and cupboard under the stringers is an attractive way to boost the interest level of an ordinary stair. In keeping with the rest of the space, though, these have a certain homemade asymmetry that pleasantly undercuts any serious furniture-making pretensions.

B

THE RAILING

It's a rope, obviously enough, threaded through a hole in the newel and knotted. Homemade? Probably. Building-code-approved? Probably not. It is, however, a clever and eyecatching touch that does a fine job of relieving the imposing heaviness of thcomes all the wood and brick in this room.

C

THE FIREPLACE

That a staircase should cleave to the hearth is certainly a worthy maxim. That a staircase should walk into a hearth is a little unorthodox. But it does have some of the same positive effect of placing a window at the end of a tight landing—it helps alleviate the sense of walking into a wall. Notice, too, the nice detail of the stairstep brickwork on the mantel.

Cozy Craftsman

Craftsman-style bungalows are some of the best expressions of Arts and Crafts values in America. A typical front entryway in this style of house features a wide oak door and a staircase hugging a side wall, allowing convenient access without overwhelming the space. Another hallmark is the relatively low first landing, allowing the master of the house to use it as an impromptu stage when the occasion calls for drama.

Gustav Stickley, founder of the Craftsman style, was committed to beautiful wood trim and surfaces, no matter how modest the house. That commitment is evident here, particularly in the beamed ceiling and the high wainscoting that continues from the doorframe and along the surrounding walls. *(Photograph, page 42)*

A

THE WINDOWS

Craftsman bungalows, for all their dark wood and massive built-in furniture, have a definite knack for letting in just the right amount of light at just the right moment. Here, small but perfectly placed casement windows relieve the dark, heavy paneling surrounding the landing and stairs as they provide good light for the entryway.

B

THE PARTITION

Instead of a traditional balustrade, bungalow stairs were often separated from the rest of the space by some sort of partition. Here, the partition begins with a tall newel. The top is left partially open to allow light to filter in from the casements along the stairway.

C

THE SETTLE

Gustav Stickley rose to fame first as a furniture maker and believed strongly in houses furnished with efficient, well thought-out, beautiful built-in furniture. In reality, Stickley was doing home organization a century before home organization stores arrived in shopping malls. A settle at the base of a staircase was commonplace. The bench is an ideal place to take off shoes, and he space beneath provides clutter-reducing storage.

Garden Wall Stair

Lots of builders today work with logs to build everything from deck stairs to entire houses, but it takes a patient craftsperson with a good eye to work with rough, irregular timbers like these. It seems like the builder deliberately chose logs for their personality rather than straightness or uniformity. Maybe he was inspired by the dry-fitted stone retaining wall or the overflowing garden. However he found his inspiration for this naturalistic curved garden stair, the result is impressive and fits in perfectly with the surrounding yard. *(Photograph, page 93)*

A BIT OF INSIGHT

This rustic staircase was conceived and constructed by Atli Arason as part of a scenic pathway near Hollywood, California. Arason included a number of similar hand-built wooden archways, bridges, benches, and other stairs along the path. They all share the same rustic Adirondack aesthetic. Rather than call attention to themselves, the structures blend in with and seem to grow quite naturally from the surrounding landscape.

A

RAILING

One wonders how long it took to find a branch with just the right curve and shape to form the railing for this stair. The railing and starting newel are a single piece, supported by one forked baluster. The bark was stripped from the railing to make a smoother handhold.

B

TREADS AND STRINGERS

When your medium is lumber, shaping stringers and joining treads to them is a matter of precise measurement. When your materials are a little less than standard, achieving precision takes a bit of creativity. Here, the gentle curve at the top is the result of a serendipitous choice of logs more than anything else. The treads and stringers are hand-notched to create a stable, solid joint. Notice how the sixth and seventh treads from the bottom have been notched on their front edges to accommodate a bow in the inside stringer. Rather than leave the ends of the treads flat, they've been carefully rounded off—further evidence of a careful craftsperson at work.

Good Design Turned Sideways

In its efficiency and simplicity, this contemporary staircase shows considerable Arts and Crafts influence along with several idiosyncratic touches of its own. The stairs are sited in the front hall along a wall—but the front wall, not the side, causing the stairs to pass directly above the front door rather than next to it. This layout is well suited for the wider façades of many contemporary houses. It also means the landing sits directly above the bumped-out entry hall, allowing proportions generous enough for a seating area. *(Photograph, page 44)*

A

THE WINDOWS

It hardly bears mentioning again, but windows do wonders for stairways. Here, light pours in through two stacked windows. The white balustrade and risers along with the light oak treads seem particularly warm and inviting in the sunlight. Another window illuminates the oversized landing, which is properly equipped with a comfortable windowseat that makes it into an ideal private, sunny seating space.

B

THE BALUSTRADE

The through-the-post rail and classical boxy newels are as attractive as always and well suited to the restrained details of the rest of the stair. The balusters are less standard. They are a simple gridwork panel, but the design that proves quite attractive when caught in the light of the windows.

C

THE FIRST FLIGHT

The extra width on the first flight is an unusual and seemingly decadent touch but, in practice, a very striking one, taking the notion of stairs-as-stage to another level. One wonders whether the designer had in mind that the extra width would create an ideal impromptu riser for extended-family photos. More practically, it provides a useful display space for potted plants.

Hanging Curve

Classically trimmed curving stairs that seem to sprout unsupported from the wall—could there be a more appealing description for the staircase connoisseur? Hardly. Curves and cantilevers are two details closely associated with the grandest of staircases in the grandest of houses, but here they adapt well to closer confines.

It's a fact, well and truly established, that attention to the smallest details pays off in even the biggest of designs. This staircase is a good example. The details here all have a classic appeal, with the added flair of bold colors. Notice the band of molding that highlights the curve of the stairwell opening, and the tastefully slender railing and balusters. From top to bottom, this stair is a home run. (*Photograph, page 49*)

A

THE WINDOW

The window at the bottom of this stair provides much more than light; it provides a sense of space at a spot that would otherwise seem cramped

B

FLOATING STAIRS

Floating stairs have been defying gravity in houses for a couple of centuries, but today, they're easier than ever to design and build (see page 54 for more information). This set of floating stairs marries with the curved wall to form a stair that is both attractive and space efficient. The stairs themselves have perfect classical proportions, including nosing that wraps all the way around the tread; the effect is of each step appearing to be a block stacked on top of the next.

C

UNDER THE STAIRS

Putting the space under cantilevered stairs to use is an obvious choice; figuring out how to do it so what goes underneath doesn't take away from the effect of the stairs is another matter. The boldly contrasting paint job on the adjacent wall is the key to this solution here, as it makes the stairs stand out strikingly. The child's table and chairs don't clutter the space, and the legs of the table are painted to match the wall, further unifying the scene.

Modern Classic

People often associate contemporary design with cold metal and glass—with objects that, though impressive, tend to be uninviting and a bit unapproachable. Not so with this stair. Here, classical forms and modern execution harmonize in a simple straight-run staircase, The light wood, finished in three subtly different tones, is warm, inviting to the eye and the touch—as a good, casual staircase should be.

Notice, too, how the first few steps overlap the columned entryway to the adjoining dining room. This seemingly small, somewhat unconventional detail is the difference between a stair that's a ramp from one floor to the next and a stair that functions as stage for grand entrances as well as seating space. *(Photograph, page 55)*

A BIT OF INSIGHT

Staircase runners are more frequently associated with nineteenth-century styles, particularly Victorian—than they are with modern aesthetics. Not all runners have heavy floral patterns and ornamental brass hardware. This staircase shows that a well-designed runner can work well in the sparer context of a modern staircase. In addition to providing an interesting visual contrast with the light wood of the stairs, the runner serves the practical purpose of saving wear and tear on the treads and dampening noise from foot traffic—and it feels great under bare feet. Runners are quite easy to install; see page 112 to learn how.

A

THE SHELF

The narrow shelf built into the wall side of the stairwell opening is a small touch, but it allows for a pleasingly clean display for small objects. In addition, it effectively relieves what is often an unbroken expanse of bare wall.

B

THE BALUSTRADE

The balustrade, though decidedly modern at first glance, is more than a little classic in its proportions. All the traditional parts—large newel with cap, thin, evenly spaced balusters, and sinuous railing—are present, though they seem to have been reduced to their bare, geometric essentials.

Neoclassical Cascade

It's hard not to be struck by the resemblance this neo-classical staircase bears to an impossibly neat and orderly waterfall. It embodies the central principles of a grand formal stair. It commands attention immediately. It defies one to make a boring, hurried entrance. Its multiple flights and generous landings demand a casual, graceful descent, with perhaps a pause to propose a toast or to greet a just-arrived guest. And why not? As not even the smallest detail has been forgotten on this stair, taking one's time isn't bad at all. *(Photograph, page 69)*

A

CANTILEVERED STAIRS

Cantilevered stairs are eternally appealing, not only for the sense of miraculous weightlessness they inevitably convey but also for the space they save. Here, all surfaces of the individual step are trimmed. Particularly effective and striking is the way the contrasting edge of each tread seems to continue all the way under the riser above, creating strong horizontal lines and giving the impression of individual stacked steps. The space under the stairs is lit inconspicuously by fixtures recessed in the undersides of the treads.

B

THE BALUSTRADE

A typical period touch, this balustrade incorporates three baluster profiles. Note how the dark mahogany finial and railing are accentuated by the white newels and balusters—an attractive touch that also allows one to be thrifty with less expensive, paint-grade components and splurge on beautiful, exotic wood for railings and accents.

C

THE STARTING STEPS

Starting steps are a common and attractive touch on almost any stair—the staircase equivalent of an open-arm welcome. Here, though, they continue the pattern of offset horizontal lines begun at the top and provide a smooth finish to the gradual waterfall of the staircase.

Singular Spiral

Contemporary isn't just a synonym for minimalism executed in gleaming metal and glass. The best contemporary design avails itself of all the opportunities presented by the enormous variety of materials available to homebuilders today. This is particularly true in staircases, which, with all their facets and features, present a glorious range of challenges to builders and architects. This grand spiral stair is a case in point. One is tempted to call this combination of rough timber, intricately worked metal, and precise engineering *neo-rustic*, but by any name, it's impressive for its seamless integration of design elements and materials. *(Photograph, page 61)*

A

THE SCONCES

Little touches not at all connected with the staircase itself can help bring off the overall effect and tie the space together. Here it's the simple iron sconces, which echo the balustrade, that seem to make it all click.

B

THE CENTRAL COLUMN

This is by no means a typical spiral-stair central column, but there's something pleasingly appropriate about a tree trunk providing the support for a spiral stair. It's a bit of a wink in the direction of the organic nature of the spiral, perhaps. A touch of human ingenuity helps carry off the effect with panache. Notice the lack of any visible support between the trunk and the slim wooden treads, making the treads seem, well, like branches.

C

THE BALUSTRADE

The balustrade on this stair is an impressive piece of craftsmanship all by itself—though it is certainly a perfect fit with the rest of the stair. The hand-worked wrought iron tree branches curve gently along with the treads, blending in naturally with the real wooden antecedents. The seemingly patternless tangle of branches is a nice change of pace from the unrelenting repetition that normally characterizes balustrades.

Stone Pathway

There's something universally appealing about building with stone. A stone patio, a stone pathway with stone steps—these strike a chord because they seem substantial and permanent, even eternal (especially if you do the hard work of actually positioning the stones). Stone also has a way of becoming part of the landscaping rather than a distraction from it, as can sometimes be the case with wooden decks.

Of course, there are also practical reasons for building with stone. Even if it's not *actually* eternal, it will far outlast any sort of wooden steps, and stone is the original no-maintenance building material—it actually gets better with age. Choosing local stone for outdoor projects ensures their seamless blend into the surrounding landscape. *(Photograph, page 97)*

A BIT OF INSIGHT

You can approach the design of a natural stone path and stairway much the way you would approach that of a garden of native plant species. Types of stone have regional qualities, just as plants and timber do. Depending on where you live, you might find locally quarried granite, flagstone, quartzite, slate, shale, or limestone. Native stone has another advantage: it is usually cheaper than stone hauled in from a distance. Check under "Stone" in your local telephone directory for local quarries and distributors. If you're persistent, you may also be able to purchase odd pieces from larger jobs for next to nothing.

A

PART OF THE SCENE

Stone integrates well with landscaping, as is particularly evident in this stone stair, which fits in naturally with the narrow, rocky garden waterfall and the stone patio. Notice the stairstep effect in the waterfall.

B

CUT STONE STEPS

Cut stone has wonderful irregularities and textures and, in most cases, is slip-resistant even when wet. Because the edge of the treads is not uniform, though, lights are essential to make a stone stairway safe to climb when the sun goes down.

Study in Curves

All staircases feature pattern and repetition to some degree, but this classic cantilevered curved stair takes the notion to another level. All so-called floating stair designs are impressive, but when all the details work together, the result is breathtaking. Considerable engineering and construction skills go into this sort of stair, so choose a staircase carpenter with care. This design has the additional benefit of being efficient in terms of floor space, perfect for making a big statement in a smaller foyer. *(Photograph, page 76)*

A

THE STAIRWELL OPENING

One of the best details of this staircase isn't on the staircase at all. Notice the opening of the stairwell, especially the curved portion opposite the top landing. The shape matches the curve of the actual stairway and the trim matches the skirtboards, almost giving the impression that the staircase was cut from the floor above and simply spiraled down to the floor. The extraordinary seamlessness and weightlessness of the staircase begins here.

B

FLOATING STAIRS

The stringers of the unsupported section of this stair are cut almost frighteningly shallow to get the maximum floating effect and to remain balanced visually with the railing and the stairwell opening. It's almost a pity to cover the framing of a curved stair like this with trim. To construct this gravity-floating flight, carpenters built the stringers of dozens of thin pieces of lumber bent around a form and laminated together. In modern construction, this is done in a workshop or factory. If you can make a trip to see the work in progress, you won't be disappointed.

C

THE BALUSTRADE

The curves continue to the very end of the stair, where the graceful ribbon of a railing terminates in a classic *volute*, which is cleverly echoed by the starting step below. Simple, straight balusters are ideal for this stair. They add very little visual weight and seem to reinforce the impossibly delicate proportions of the staircase as a whole.

Classic Craftsman

There's no mistaking Craftsman-style stairs. They are marvels of understated detail, beautiful materials, and exquisite craftsmanship. Unlike more formal designs, Craftsman staircases emphasize horizontal lines and feel more cozy than awe-inspiring (though when one looks closely, the attention to detail is frequently cause for amazement). A staircase like this one is most at home in a bungalow, but any homeowner who appreciates simple beauty and warm materials should consider a Craftsman design. *(Photograph, page 45)*

A

THE BALUSTRADE

Arts and Crafts, or Craftsman, balustrades often eschew more traditional turned-spindle balusters for designs with a distinctly Far Eastern influence. The balusters are simple square posts (echoing the massive rectilinear newels) but are arranged to create a subtle picture frame effect.

B

THE SETTLE

Built-in furniture is a hallmark of good Craftsman design. It helps fight clutter, and its characteristically solid construction appeals to the Craftsman sensibility. A settle built in at the foot of a stairway is a particularly fine touch. This design integrates beautifully with the rest of the room, seamlessly connecting the columned entry on the left side with the first flight of the staircase.

In contemporary houses, the appeal of the staircase settle is much as it was a century ago. The settle helps transform an entry hall from an open, uninviting space into a comfortable, human-scaled space. Like so many Craftsman details, though, the settle does double duty. These elegant benches frequently serve as linen chests; their seats are hinged and opened to storage space below.

A BIT OF INSIGHT

At the beginning of the twentieth century, American furniture maker and designer Gustav Stickley began publishing *The Craftsman*. This magazine was dedicated to Stickley's unique interpretation of the Arts and Crafts movement, which had emerged decades earlier in England. Stickley championed simplicity and exquisite craftsmanship, decrying the shoddy mass-produced furniture being produced in the United States at the time. Craftsmanship wasn't just an aesthetic, Stickley insisted, but a lifestyle. In *The Craftsman* he published everything from articles on philosophy and poetry to plans for bookcases and even entire houses. The staircase featured on this page, with its rectangular balustrade motif, is strongly reminiscent of a design featured in the November 1906 issue of *The Craftsman*.

Elegant Stairs in a Flawed Space

This *L*-shaped stair presents intriguing and elegant solutions to an imperfect space. The space is really too tight for the *L* layout. The width of the useful portion of the lower flight is quite a bit less than the second flight and is certainly less than optimal. A straight stair would be no better, though, as it would either overlap the door or be very steep. Even as an *L*, the stair comes a bit too close to the front door, which is immediately to the right of the first flight. Even so, because of its careful design, no one would ever think this staircase ill-proportioned or unattractive. *(Photograph, page 20)*

A

THE SCREEN

Some sort of partition is in order between the staircase and the entryway to the immediate right. Instead of a traditional railing, which would make the landing seem to loom too much over the too-close front door, this stair has a wooden screen that provides just enough visual separation but stops short of seeming like an actual wall.

B

THE BALUSTERS

The balusters continue the stairstep pattern that begins in the picture-frame molding on the wall (which simply but effectively lends visual interest to an otherwise blank expanse). They're also attached to the treads in an unusual and fascinating way, with the horizontal slat extending directly from the edge of each tread and the vertical slat from the top front.

C

THE FIRST FLIGHT

By extending the width of the first flight all the way across the run of the second flight, the designer has effectively concealed the narrowness of the useful portion of the flight. The extended stairs also balance the upper flight beautifully and make attractive use of what would otherwise be dead space between the first flight and the far wall.

Rough-Hewn Timber

Few real frontier log cabins actually had stairs; a ladder
to the sleeping loft was normally the best means of ascent
one could hope for. Today's log cabin homes are rarely
so limited. But you needn't live in a log cabin to appreciate this substantial log staircase (though it doesn't hurt if
you do). Staircases built of rough-hewn timbers look
good in everything from small cabins to new, large, post-
and-beam houses.

Contractors who specialize in log-style construction
are common and they offer custom or semi-custom staircases for surprisingly affordable prices. Check your local
telephone directory for listings. Logs are also excellent
alternatives to plain lumber for stairs and railings on
decks so keep them in mind for outdoor stairs too.
(Photograph, page 81)

A

THE WINDOW

It's hard to imagine how much difference a little window can make until you
try to picture what the bottom of this
stair without one. The lower landing is
relatively small, but the addition of the
window provides light and relieves the
unpleasant sensation of walking into a
log wall.

B

OPEN-TREAD STAIRS

In addition to providing an open feeling and allowing in more light from
the nearby windows, the open risers of
a log staircase show all the character of
the individual logs. The actual load-
bearing members are almost never visible in standard staircase construction,
but not here, where massive twin log
posts serve as stringers.

C

THE BALUSTRADE

The builders arranged the railing so
one of the support posts, rather than a
newel, could receive the ends of the
railing—which is, not surprisingly, a
log. Obviously, delicate turned balusters just wouldn't do for this rustic
staircase. Small, curvy logs stand at a
sort of irregular attention to complete
the baluster.

Modern Geometry

This modern stair has a rather unusual situation relative to the front door. It is a fairly typical *L*-shaped structure, but rotated such that its second flight rises directly above the front entryway. This provides convenient access to the mezzanine directly above and challenges the aesthetics of the rest of the entryway.

Open risers are a critical factor in making this arrangement work. They make the back of the staircase far less monolithic and allow light into the entryway. It's also imperative in such a layout that all facets of the staircase be finished, as they'll all be regularly in view .

The materials are fairly characteristic of this sort of modern staircase—a combination of the beauty of simple wood forms with the strength of metal. Carpet wrapped around the whole tread is an unusual touch that makes the treads not only soft underfoot but also very quiet—a treatment that's worth consideration when steps adjoin a bedroom. *(Photograph, page 51)*

A BIT OF INSIGHT

Staircases and modernism have a long and interesting relationship. Marcel Duchamp's 1912 painting *Nude Descending a Staircase* helped jump-start modernism in the United States. On the other hand, the single most pervasive examples of vernacular modern architecture—the ranch and the skyscraper—seem to strike a blow against everything stairs stand for, replacing them with streamlined single-story living or with elevators. The great American modern architect Philip Johnson famously claimed that stairs, along with chairs and city squares, were the hardest things to design. He may be right, but every important modern architect, from Frank Lloyd Wright to Le Corbusier to Mies van der Rohe, made a staircase a central feature of their major buildings.

A

THE BALUSTRADE

It goes without saying that staircases depend on pattern and repetition, but this staircase takes these essential ideas to an extreme. The stairstep railing, a pleasing echo of the stairs themselves, also helps make the line of sight from the entryway more appealing by creating an appealing pattern.

B

THE SUPPORTING BEAMS

By using the same materials and finishes, the designer has artfully integrated the beams that support both the stairs and part of the mezzanine leading to the staircase.

Outgoing Enclosure

An enclosed staircase is probably the least heralded of all stair types. No wonder, as it lacks the three-dimensional interest, the grand balustrade, and the view of a stair with at least one open side—definitely not the first choice of a stair connoisseur. Of course, this need not be the case. Enclosed stairs offer opportunities despite their limitations. Part of the problem with a conventional enclosed staircase is that the walls prevent it from opening up at the bottom, making the transition from hall to stairs abrupt and uninviting. The stairs almost always seem self-contained and uninvolved with the rest of the room. This stair design offers several useful solutions for problematic enclosed stairs. *(Photograph, page 78)*

A

THE RAILING

Rather than end at the edge of the walls as most railings do, these wrap around the wall, spilling out and following the line of the starting steps. This shows the carved hardwood railing to good effect and also helps reinforce the overall sense of openness to the surrounding space.

B

STAIRS TO DEFINE SPACE

The stairs in these rooms are an excellent example of how stairs can provide definition and connection for open space. Lowering a floor just a few feet is a classic technique for defining a space, and it works well here to separate the entryway from the family room. The identical floor and tread finishes along with the white risers on all the stairs help provide a sense of flow through all the rooms.

C

STARTING STEPS

The key feature of this staircase is its placement a few feet out from the walls—a small touch that effectively integrates what would have been a completely separate stair with the surrounding space. By beginning the staircase outside the walls, the architect was able to create three gently tapering starting steps. These make the transition from the entryway to the stairwell much more gradual—and the stairs gain a bit of the stage quality that is so important to a good front staircase. With the the main stair drawn forward a few feet, the starting steps can also flow naturally into the two steps that lead to the slightly sunken family room. The starting-step taper actually begins with the first step up from the family room.

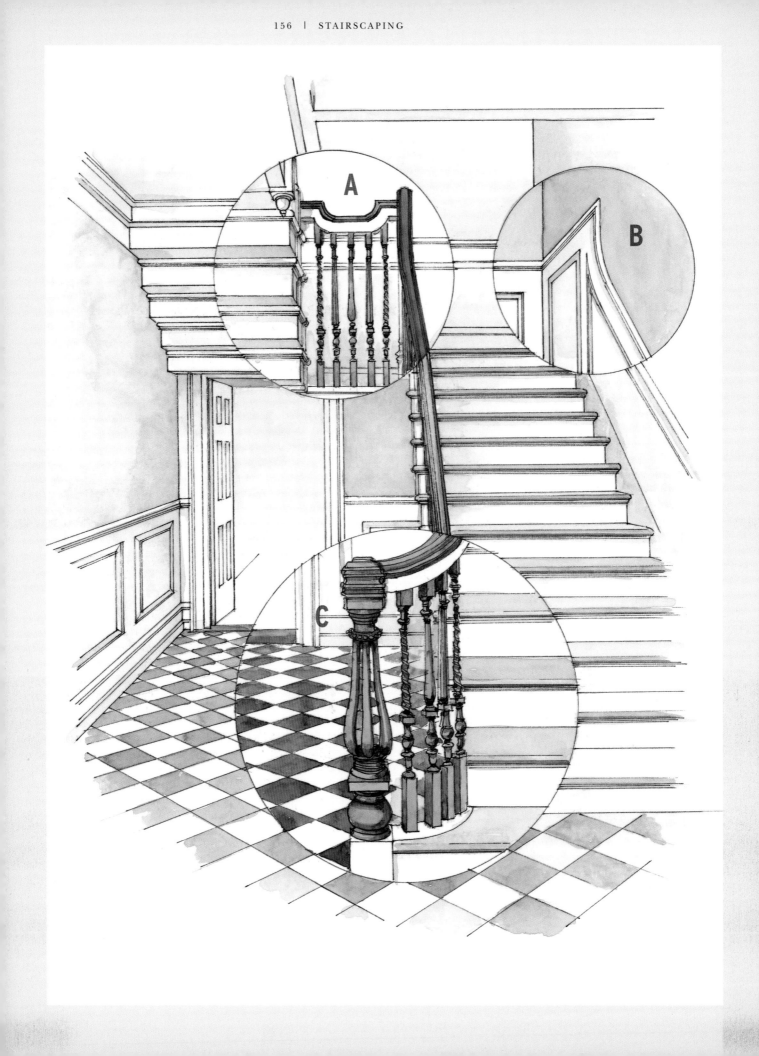

A Well-Trimmed Switchback

From the molding on the edges of the treads to the curved starting step to the graceful dip in the railing on the landing, this switchback staircase is full of magnificent details. No single detail is particularly extravagant or overwhelming, though; like all good design, the parts work together to create a harmonious whole. *(Photograph, page 36)*

A

THE SECOND FLIGHT

More often than not, the underside of the second flight of a switchback stair is finished flat, maybe with a bit of paneling. The only evidence of the stairs above is the slope of the ceiling. The builder of this stair, going a different route, has trimmed and finished the underside of the second flight so that each stair is defined from the bottom, complete with matching crown molding. It seems as if the individual stairs are floating against the wall. This is no mean feat for the carpenter, as it involves cutting a sawtooth pattern into both sides of the stringer, but the standout effect is unique and one that any staircase aficionado will appreciate.

B

THE SHADOW RAIL

One effective way to add visual interest to a staircase is to build a shadow railing. On this stair, the paneling on the wall opposite the balustrade is capped with trim that follows the line of the rail, even shadowing its upward curve at the landing. Almost any sort of wall molding or paneling can be used to create a shadow railing. One common technique is to continue wainscoting and a chair rail up the staircase wall (as shown here).

C

THE BALUSTRADE

Where is it written that every baluster must be the same? This balustrade has three subtly different baluster patterns. Far from looking unnatural, the effect is understated but visually interesting. On most staircases, balusters are reasonably easy to remove and replace (newels and railings are a job for pros, though). If you have simple straight balusters or several loose or damaged balusters, you might consider replacing some or all of them. Home centers generally sell several patterns. If you can find two or three that vary just slightly as shown here, you might create a pattern. If you want to be more adventurous, you can head to an architectural salvage yard (with your old baluster measurements in hand!) and see whether you can find a few beautiful old balusters. If you're really lucky, you'll find a carved newel as gorgeous and intricate as the one on this balustrade.

Garden Spiral

One design concept making a welcome comeback in home construction is the outdoor room. Homeowners are increasingly insisting on exterior spaces that flow naturally from the interior. The popularity of multilevel decks, porches, and solariums, the rise of the full-fledged outdoor kitchen as an essential home improvement—all of these trends are evidence of the blurring of the boundaries between indoors and out. People want to extend livable space outdoors rather than shut the house off from it.

One way to facilitate this extension of space is with a staircase more traditionally associated with interiors. This simple steel spiral—inexpensively available as a do-it-yourself kit—connects the second-story terrace and the ground-level patio, making passage between the two spaces as convenient outdoors as in. No doubt, on cool summer evenings, stairs like these become a destination in themselves, reminiscent of urban fire-escape balconies. *(Photograph, page 99)*

A BIT OF INSIGHT

Metal spiral stair kits are fairly easy to add to existing second-story decks and balconies. When done right, they can look down-right fantastic. But if you're planning a new deck, or if you're looking for a way to seamlessly add a spiral to an existing deck, many deck builders will build spirals to match the style of the main decking. This means using the same wood (or composite) decking for the treads as for the rest of the deck and matching the railings to the deck's rails. The result is a staircase that increases access to the deck without looking added on.

A

ADDING ON

Because spiral stairs have such a small footprint, they needn't dominate the patio or yard. Adding a spiral to an existing balcony is as simple as creating a solid platform for the bottom and an opening in the railing at the top. By running this kit-built spiral next to the terrace, the builder just had to leave an opening in the terrace railing where the spiral's built-in landing ended.

B

BLENDING IN

One of the hallmarks of a good indoor stair is a smooth relationship with the surrounding room. Similarly, here, the bold red finish on the spiral blends in rather than shouts out among the greenery of the garden.

Minimal Approach

This archetypal modern staircase is smooth, sleek, and elegant, as cool as the polished concrete floor beneath it. Like so much modern design, this stair takes a broad view of which materials and textures work well in a house. The main part of the staircase is built from wood, but there are no embellishments or ornaments aside from the pure lines of the structure itself. The impression is decidedly minimalist but also engaging and interesting.

This staircase also evinces careful engineering that allows it to occupy only a small portion of the stairwell, the majority of which remains visually open and uncluttered by support structures. The landing is particularly attractive, as it places nothing between the users and the glass. *(Photograph, page 47)*

A

OPEN RISERS

Open risers are something of a given in a great many contemporary staircases. In this stair, though, there is no question that they are the best choice. The structure of the staircase is actually quite substantial and dark, but by leaving the risers open, much of the light from the massive window that makes up the back wall of the stairwell reaches the surrounding space. As a result, the impression one gets is of a light and open space—a highly satisfying effect.

B

THE BALUSTRADE

Glass is a favorite material in much of the architecture of the last seventy-five years—and with good reason, given its enormous flexibility and utility. The huge window certainly attests to the power of glass to transform a space, but the glass panels that make up the balustrade on the staircase are equally important to the design, as they are at once substantial and transparent. The panels admit light from the window but also seem in proportion to the massive wooden stringers to which they're attached.

A BIT OF INSIGHT

American architect Stephen Ehrlich designed this staircase for a house in Pacific Palisades, California. Ehrlich practices a unique brand of modernism; he is clearly faithful to the modernist values of clean lines and simple, geometric forms, but he also values diversity and eclecticism. This is perhaps an outgrowth of six years spent in Africa, including a term in the Peace Corps, where he was the first western architect to work in Marrakech, Morocco.

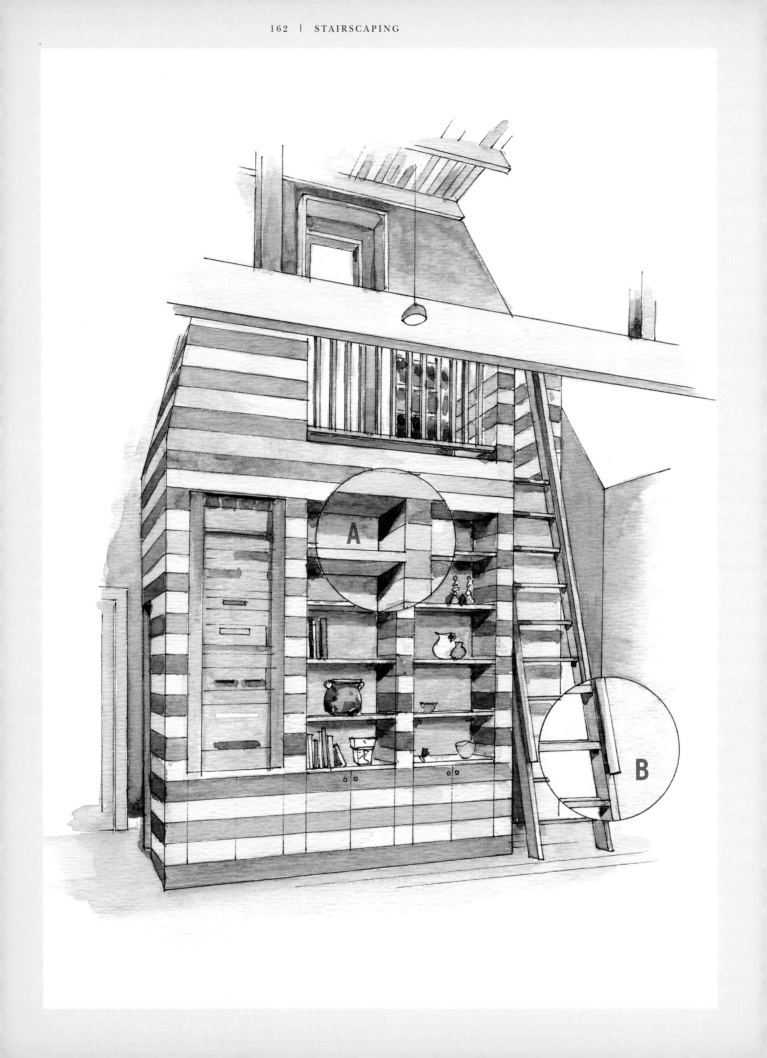

Ladder to a Loft

Some spaces just can't be reached by stairs. When ladders become part of the picture, though, small, elevated spaces present new opportunities for lofted mini-rooms, such as offices, arts and crafts workspaces, or just secluded, quiet hiding places. And not just in urban apartments, either: the trend toward great rooms and other multistory spaces in houses presents a variety of opportunities for lofting.

In this example, what would otherwise be wasted space on top of a massive media center and shelving unit became an ideal small office space after the homeowners allowed for a ladder. An indulgently large window helps make the space an attractive place to work—or just sit and ponder.

A permanent ladder doesn't have much in common with the wobbly thing you might climb to clean out the gutters in the fall. This ladder is beautifully crafted and finished to match the surrounding woodwork. It's also firmly attached at the top to eliminate any chance of tipping. *(Photograph, page 64)*

A BIT OF INSIGHT

Not every ladder needs a destination. Even if you don't have a loft space, a permanent ladder can be a useful and attractive addition to a room. Library ladders are set in tracks to provide convenient and constant access to stored objects. Traditionally, of course, library ladders provide access to tall bookcases in large libraries. There is no rule that a library ladder can only be used in a library, though. Permanent, movable ladders can open new frontiers of usable space in large rooms by providing quick access to shelves in kitchens, great rooms, home offices, and anywhere else where raised storage would be useful.

A

SHELVES

The ladder was custom-built along with the shelving unit. Because it shares the same fine materials, it blends in quite inconspicuously.

B

RAILINGS

A handrail is as useful a touch on a ladder as it is on a staircase. Handrails a few inches above the ladder frame make the descent much easier.

A Hand Up

Lofts and converted attics seem to bring out the creative, clever side of stairs. Maybe the reason is the space itself, or budgetary constraints, but it seems as though nontraditional spaces inspire the most nontraditional, dramatic, and interesting designs. This one is no exception. It offers a good solution to the too-massive stair in a small space. Much of the mass of regular staircases comes from the widely spaced stringers necessary when building with traditional lumber. A steel I-beam, as used here, has no such requirement; a single beam is more than up to the task of carrying a few stairs.

The I-beam isn't the only eclectic element of this postmodern stair. The designer has given the stair a homemade feel by pressing a variety of objects into service as components, from steel pipe used as full-height newels to a streetlight to an inventive adaptation of a simple art supply store mannequin. *(Photograph, page 53)*

A BIT OF INSIGHT

This staircase is located in Boston on the first floor of an 1888 one-room schoolhouse that was converted to a residence in the 1960s. The first-floor classroom was divided into living spaces and a kitchen. The most recent owners decided to take a cue from the building's one-room roots and de-converted the first floor, creating an open, loft-like space. This left them with a problem: how to build a stair to the second floor without disturbing all the openness. The steel and hardwood solution to the staircase problem—dubbed "the Flying Stair" by the owners—was fabricated from locally milled lumber and metal procured from a local auto body shop.

A

THE STAIRS AND STRINGER

The I-beam stringer is actually available for this exact application, so you needn't raid a nearby construction site. The treads are sections of prefabricated butcher block cut to look like old skateboards. With a generous coat of polyurethane, they'll be hardwearing and eyecatching. They're attached to the I-beam with nothing more than welded steel brackets.

B

RAILINGS

This book has stressed more than a few times how important it is that a staircase should seem welcoming and make you want to climb it. Here, with the creative application of a couple of wooden artists' hand models to the railings on this loft staircase, the designer has clearly taken this advice to heart. The railings literally reach out to offer a hand up.

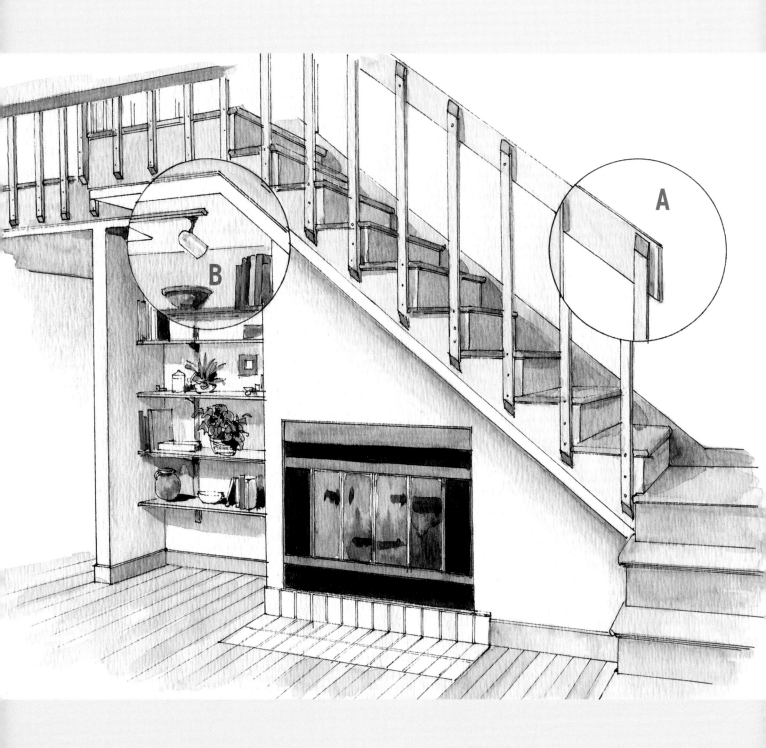

Contemporary Casual

Staircases in vernacular houses—practical buildings with minimal design elements—were often built adjacent to a fireplace. No surprise there; the hearth was the center of the home, and it made perfect sense that the staircase be convenient to it. For contemporary casual lifestyles, this layout still makes a good deal of sense. Even if the house doesn't have a central fireplace, it probably has a room in which the family likes to gather. A staircase that adjoins this space will naturally be useful.

This warm, wooden *L*-shaped stair makes a strong case for situating the staircase in common area instead of a foyer. Rather than stand aloof, it seems to wrap around the family room, with its lower flight conveniently placed to provide a bit of extra seating near the fire. *(Photograph, page 87)*

A BIT OF INSIGHT

Built-ins are a hallmark of Craftsman-style homes. Bookcases, benches, cabinets, closets, and even bathrooms proliferated in the spaces around and beneath staircases. Modern home designs can take inspiration from the Craftsman style while addressing modern needs and developments. A fireplace under a formal front hall staircase is an unusual and pleasant touch. Imagine greeting guests on cold evening with a roaring fire. Modern zero-clearance direct-vent fireplaces can make this possible. They require none of the complicated brickwork or chimneys that traditional fireplaces do, making retrofit additions simple.

For more casual environments, the space under a stair can be an excellent location for a built-in entertainment center, especially if you use a flat-screen television. This arrangement works particularly well in remodeled basements.

A

THE BALUSTRADE

The best balustrade for a casual staircase is often the simplest, the one that makes the stairs approachable. This one is crafted from lumber that matches the treads and the floorboards. The only decoration is the subtle bevel at the end of each board.

B

THE FIREPLACE AND SHELVES

Built-ins such as shelves and benches have long helped make staircases focal points for casual rooms. Here, a simple set of shelves yields an efficient display and storage space, a worthy substitute for the more traditional mantel. Modern gas fireplaces can add another attention-gathering dimension. They do not require the large and complex flues of the wood-burning fireplaces of years past—making it easier to build them into tight spaces, such as under a set of stairs. The cantilevered portion of the stairs overhangs the fireplace and enhances the general sense of comfort and enclosure.

An Outdoor Stair with Indoor Flair

It's a rare house that presents an opportunity for a long flight of exterior stairs; most lots simply aren't big enough. This is one of the fortunate few, and its staircase takes advantage of a generous run with subtle, interior-style details and fine construction.

The stringers of this staircase are the concrete walls, an ideal choice for a long-lived stair in any climate. To attach the treads and the balustrade securely, metal fasteners were embedded in the concrete after it was poured.

This example also demonstrates good proportions. As a general rule, short front stairs need to be wider than the standard 36 inches (1 m) in order to look balanced, but when the flight is longer, proportions more like those of an interior stair tend to look better. *(Photograph, page 98)*

A BIT OF INSIGHT

In almost all climates, horizontal wooden surfaces on exterior structures are a bad idea. Pooling water on staircase treads not only encourages rot but also can make the stairs slippery. Most deck stairs have open risers and a slight gap between the two tread boards for just these reasons. Closed riser stairs with solid treads, like the one illustrated, require a bit more care in design; otherwise, water will pool on the treads, especially at the joint between tread and riser. To address this problem, make sure the treads are built with a slight downward slope to encourage drainage. Your local building code may mandate a specific slope.

A

THE RISERS

It's nearly impossible to maintain unpainted wood on an outdoor stair; some sort of heavy-duty exterior paint is almost always in order. On a long set of stairs, this can have the unfortunate effect of presenting a person standing at the bottom with a wall of a single color—rather dull indeed. To relieve this, the architect has taken the simple but attractive step of cutting star shapes from the risers.

B

THE BALUSTRADE

Neoclassical balustrade details look elegant and substantial inside but also work quite well outside, as this stair shows. The wide railing and the substantial, box-shaped newels stand out against their heavy concrete foundations and are a compelling alternative to more traditional cast iron.

Sunny Back Stair

A narrow back stair or basement staircase in an old farm-house or Victorian house can be a sad, dark, neglected thing—a poor stepsister to the fancier foyer stairs. This is too bad, because such stairs often have the potential to be quite useful. This enclosed stair, for example, is simple but very well done. Ample light keeps it from being a dull passageway. Bright yellow beadboard adds a nice country touch and contributes to the overall lightness and warmth of the stair. The unpainted treads are well worn and pleasing to the eye, especially against the traditional whitewashed risers. *(Photograph, page 101)*

A

WINDOWS

Smartly placed windows can make a narrow staircase seem much less confining. They'll let in light no matter where they're placed along the flight, but some spots have additional benefits. Because the top and bottom landings of these stairs are reached by doors situated perpendicular to the flight, windows opposite the doors are a particularly good choice, as they eliminate the unpleasant sensation of walking into a wall.

B

THE RAILING

The bracket-mounted wall railing is almost as traditionally maligned and neglected as the basement stairs. Many a homeowner has attached one just long enough to pass inspection and then ripped it down as soon as the inspector was out the door. This is a pity because the brackets allow you to use just about anything as a railing, as long as it's straight and sturdy. Here, a birch branch adds a bit of flair to this otherwise subdued space. It also echoes the wrought-iron branches of the wall sconce.

A BIT OF INSIGHT

Though not every tree branch is a handrail in the rough, it takes only a bit of work to turn a long, straight, newly fallen branch into a railing guaranteed to add a touch of cabin style to any staircase. The branch shown here is actually the trunk of a birch tree, but large trees may produce individual branches long enough to serve as railings. Avoid branches that appear rotten or that have been lying on the ground for more than a day or two.

You can use a branch, bark and all, and mount it with standard hardware, as shown in the illustration. You can also strip the bark off the branch for a smoother look (kind of like the walking sticks you made in camp as a kid).

Spiral with Style

Most metal spiral stairs installed in houses today are built from kits, and this highly ornamental number is no exception. It's an impressive example of how well crafted and well integrated a prefabricated spiral stair can be. Further, its site is shows how useful a spiral can be in a large, multistory room like this great room. In many houses, the main staircase is some distance away from the heavily used family spaces. A spiral stair can provide quick access to second-story bedrooms without taking up much floor space. And, of course, an attractive spiral stair is a decorative element in itself.

On this spiral, ornamental steel closely duplicates the look of wrought iron, even on the center post, but it is much easier to install. The open webbing of the treads, easily kept clean, is an attractive alternative to wood. A bit of contrast comes in the form of the brass railing. *(Photograph, page 62)*

A BIT OF INSIGHT

Ironwork and brass were important elements of Victorian staircase design. New factory technology enabled mass-production of ironwork balusters and handrails and brass ornaments that were once available only to the wealthy. Since then, manufacturing has only improved. This spiral is heavily influenced by Victorian design but is made possible by modern technology. Actually built of cast aluminum, this staircase and others like it are finished to look antique. Aluminum allows the manufacturer precise control and flexibility during manufacturing, resulting in a more precise stair, a better fit—and a lower price.

A

THE LANDING

Most spiral stairs can be mounted either directly under the second story with a stairwell opening or adjacent to the edge of a second-story space, as shown here. A matching landing deck and railing complements the treads. This type of installation is particularly dramatic in a large room.

B

THE CENTER POST

A strong central post carries the entire load of a spiral staircase and provides a mounting surface for the treads. In this kit, the central post is as good-looking as it is hardworking. The steel spacers between the brackets that hold the treads in place were forged to look like ornamental iron, giving the whole piece a substantial appearance.

Glossary

Arts and Crafts: A design movement that began in Great Britain in the late nineteenth century. Often considered a backlash against Victorian ornamentation, the Arts and Crafts aesthetic is simpler in design, with greater emphasis on materials and craftsmanship.

Back stair: Colloquial term for a second staircase in a house, typically or originally intended for servants.

Balusters: Vertical members that support the RAILING. Balusters are generally made of wood, often with decorative carving; less frequently, they are made of metal.

Balustrade: The assembly comprising the railing or banister, the BALUSTERS, the NEWEL, and the RAILING.

Cap: A decorative finial placed on top of a newel.

Carriages: See STRINGERS.

Closed stair: A staircase enclosed on both sides by full-height walls. RAILINGS are attached to either wall with brackets.

Fillet: The thin piece of wood used as a spacer between the tops of BALUSTERS.

Headroom: The distance between the edge of the opening in the upper story and the stair tread directly below. If headroom is inadequate, taller users must duck.

Landing: A horizontal platform between two flights of a staircase. Typically, a landing is the point at which a stairway changes directions.

L-shaped: A stair layout that consists of two flights at right angles to each other and a landing in between. Typically, the first flight is short and projects into a room, while the longer second flight follows a wall.

Newel or Newel post: Typically larger in diameter than balusters, newels support the ends of a railing at the top and bottom and on the landings of a staircase.

Nosing: The front edge of a TREAD. Nosing is typically milled with a round profile.

Open riser: A stair type where the vertical space between TREADS is open.

Over-the-post: A handrail arrangement in which the RAILING is a continuous piece of material that passes over the BALUSTERS and NEWELS.

Post-to-post: A handrail arrangement in which the RAILING passes through the newels instead of over them.

Railing: A long strip of material running parallel to the stairs; used as a handhold while climbing stairs. Typically, a railing is made of wood or metal and supported by BALUSTERS and NEWELS.

Rise: The vertical distance that a stair covers.

Riser: The vertical portion of a step. Generally, the rise is a vertical board that fills the space between one TREAD and the next. In some stairs, no riser board is used; these are called OPEN RISER stairs.

Run: The horizontal distance that a stair covers.

Skirtboards: Decorative lumber that covers the open portion of stringers, often finished with carving or molding.

Spiral stair: A space-efficient stair design in which a helix of stairs rises around a central column.

Staircase: The complete stair assembly, including the stairs, balustrade, and surrounding walls.

Stairwell: The volume that a staircase occupies.

Starting step: A first step (tread and riser) that is wider than the subsequent steps of a staircase. Typically, the NEWEL sits on the starting step.

Stringers: The wide framing members that carry the treads of a staircase. Typically, stringers are made of lumber notched in a stairstep pattern to support the TREADS. Two or more stringers are arranged in parallel to form a complete staircase. In some stringers, treads are inserted in grooves, called *dados*, instead of on notches; these stringers are called *housed stringers*.

Switchback: A stair arrangement in which a second flight turns 180 degrees from the first flight, typically at a landing.

Tread: The horizontal member on a staircase; the part on which one walks.

Volute: A common decorative BALUSTRADE treatment in which the handrail makes a spiral curve away from the stairs before terminating at the starting newel.

Winder: A series of turning steps in an L-SHAPED or SWITCHBACK staircase. Typically, winders are used instead of landings where space is critical.

Resources

AF Staircase Systems Limited
Heckmondwike
West Yorkshire
United Kingdom
0192.441.1188
www.afstaircases.com

Arcways
Neenah, WI USA
800.588.5096
www.arcways.com

Bisca
Helmsley
North Yorkshire
United Kingdom
0143.977.1702
www.bisca.co.uk

CinderWhit & Co.
Wahpeton, ND USA
800.527.9064
www.cinderwhit.com

Haldane UK Ltd.
Glenrothes Fife
Scotland
0159.277.5656
www.haldaneuk.com

Hardwood Design Inc.
Boca Raton, FL USA
877.315.0016
www.hardwooddesign.com

The Iron Shop
Broomall, PA USA
800.523.7427
www.theironshop.com

Mad River Woodworks
Blue Lake, CA USA
07.668.5671
www.madriverwoodworks.com

Olde Good Things
New York, NY USA
888.551.7333
www.oldegoodthings.com

Outwater
Wood-Ridge, NJ USA
800.688.9283
www.outwater.com

Piedmont Stairs
Gordonsville, VA USA
800.622.3399
www.piedmontstairs.com

Ravenwood Stairways
Alberton, P.E.I, Canada
902.853.3037
www.ravenwoodstairways.com

Roes Stair Company
Port Huron, MI USA
888.339.3321
www.roes-stairs.com

Roes Stair Company
Mt. Brydges, Ontario Canada
888.339.3321
www.roes-stairs.com

Salter Industries
Collegeville, PA USA
800.368.8280
www.salterspiralstair.com

Southern Staircase
Alpharetta, GA USA
800.874.8408
www.southernstaircase.com

Spiral Manufacturing
Baton Rouge, LA USA
800.535.9956
www.spiralstair.com

Stair Supplies
Goshen, IN USA
866.226.6536
www.stairsupplies.com

Stair World, Inc.
Ottawa, Ontario
Canada
800.387.7711
www.stairworld.com

Staircase & Millwork Co.
Alpharetta, GA USA
800.878.9778
www.mrstair.com

Staircase Solutions
Shipley West Yorkshire
United Kingdom
01274 530331
www.staircase.co.uk

Stairway Manufacturer's Association
Westminster, MA USA
800.500.5759
www.stairways.org

Westfire Manufacturing
Aurora, OR USA
800.692.6996
www.westfiremfg.com

Accessibility

Brooks Stairlifts UK
0800.834.730
www.stairlifts.co.uk

Bruno Independent Living Aids
Oconomowoc, WI USA
800.882.8183
www.bruno.com

The Center for Universal Design
Raleigh, NC. USA
919.515.3082
www.design.ncsu.edu/cud

Easystep Stairlifts Ltd
Unit 14 Hill Lane Close
Markfield Leicestershire
United Kingdom
0800.0936.911
www.easystepstairlifts.co.uk/

Just Stairlifts Limited
Woodside
Lane End Surrey
United Kingdom
0800.083.0513
www.applegate.co.uk/company
National Resource Center on Supportive
Housing and Home Modification
Los Angeles, CA USA
213.740.1364
www.homemods.org

Residential Elevators, Inc.
Crawfordville, FL USA
800.832.2004
www.residentialelevators.com

Photographer Credits

Austin Patterson Disston Architects,
    LLC/Fred George, 95; 98
Austin Patterson Disston Architects,
    LLC/Jeff McNamara, 109
Courtesy of Bruno Independent Living
    Aids, Inc./www.bruno.com, 66
Courtesy of Conant Custom Brass/
    www.conantcustombrass.com, 74
Courtesy of Creative Publishing
    International, 27; 102; 104; 105; 106
Tony Giammarino/Giammarino &
    Dworkin, 49
Tria Giovan, 20; 35
Reto Guntli/zapaimages, 54
Chipper Hatter, 92; 110
Courtesy of The Iron Shop/
    www.theironshop.com, 28; 62; 90
Douglas Keister/www.keisterphoto.com,
    42; 43; 45; 77; 80; 81 (bottom); 83; 85;
    87 (left); 93
Shelley Metcalf, 94
Eric Roth, 2; 6; 7 (top); 19; 53

Eric Roth/Susan Sargent, Design, 115
Agi Simões/zapaimages, 52
Tim Street-Porter, 13; 38; 47; 51; 56; 57
Brian Vanden Brink, 7 (bottom, right); 8;
    22; 24; 33; 36; 37; 59; 63; 72; 73; 76; 84;
    96; 99
Brian Vanden Brink/John Gillespie,
    Architect, 31
Brian Vanden Brink/Dominic Mercadante,
    Architect, 40
Brian Vanden Brink/John Morris
    Architects, 41
Brian Vanden Brink/Tom Catalano
    Architects, 44; 69
Brian Vanden Brink/Scot Simons
    Architects, 55
Brian Vanden Brink/Jack Silverio,
    Architect, 59
Brian Vanden Brink/Steven Blatt
    Architects, 64; 65
Todd Caverly/Brian Vanden Brink
    Photography, Bartolomeo Associates, 71

Brian Vanden Brink/John Libby
    Barnbuilders, 75
Brian Vanden Brink/Julie Snow
    Architects, 79
Brian Vanden Brink/Whitten-Winkleman
    Architects, 81 (top)
Brian Vanden Brink/John Cole,
    Architect, 86
Brian Vanden Brink/Warren Hall,
    Architect, 78; 87 (right)
Brian Vanden Brink/Orcutt Associates, 89
Brian Vanden Brink/Robinson & Grisaru
    Architects, 91
Brian Vanden Brink/John Morris
    Architects, 97
Brian Vanden Brink/Coastal Design
    Consultants, 101
Conrad White/zapaimages, 10
Scot Zimmerman, 61

Illustrations by Robert Leanna II

About the Author

Andrew Karre has written about home improvement and design topics from lighting to wiring. He holds degrees in English literature and music performance from Lawrence University in Appleton, Wisconsin. He has edited books for children and young adults as well as titles on business and management. Currently, he works as a book editor, specializing in home improvement and construction books. He has a longstanding interest in all aspects of architecture and construction, but his particular fixation at the moment is a 1912 bungalow in St. Paul, Minnesota, where he resides with his wife and writes. Their house happens to have a lovely switchback staircase with white oak treads and railings and a large window on the landing.